DEATH

CAME

QUICKLY

J. HANNAH LLOYD

DEATH

CAME

QUICKLY

J. HANNAH LLOYD

J. Hannah Lloyd

This is book three in the *Seasons of Courage* series. Names and locations are simply products of the author's imagination.

J. Hannah Lloyd

Dedicated to our family
who misses Matthew
every single day

J. Hannah Lloyd

Contents

Preface

When my twenty-two year old son was killed in a car crash in 2004, I did not know what to do. Never before had I experienced such devastation. The confusion, shock, and disbelief were overwhelming as I struggled to grasp the reality of what had just happened.

At that moment I decided to keep a record of my journey, not realizing God had a plan to use my loss as reinforcement for the brokenhearted. And, by writing this book, my journey through grief has a destination.

—J. HANNAH LLOYD

J. Hannah Lloyd

"Grieve, mourn and wail. Change your laughter to mourning and your joy to gloom" *(James 4:9)*

J. Hannah Lloyd

Introduction

Life beyond Foliage

"...there is hope for a tree: If it is cut down, it will sprout again, and its new shoots will not fail" *(Job 14: 7)*

"Here Mom, these are for you." Grinning from ear to ear, my vivacious teenage son shoved a dish garden full of tiny shriveled plants into my hands. "The store manager threw them away," he said. "I thought you might want them."

But the plants were so withered I had serious doubts they would survive. However, Matt had given them to me; so I drenched them all with water and hoped for the best.

Then, to my amazement and his delight, a little attention triggered those dying plants to sprout new leaves. Vibrant foliage was soon growing from all five. And every day thereafter, those lush, colorful leaves filled my kitchen with the freshness of life.

A vast amount of time has now passed since those special plants were given to me. Untold anguish and rivers of tears have streamed beneath life's bridge. Matthew was killed in a car crash over ten years ago. Yet some of the plants he'd insisted I take are still alive, and growing.

Even now, when I look at the fullness of their beauty, I realize my son continues to exist. And there is hope for our reunion because life never ends. It just transplants to another place.

J. Hannah Lloyd

Chapter One

Losing my Son

A piercing shrill instantly jarred me into a semiconscious state. My mind, still heavy with sleep, struggled to comprehend my rude awakening. Had the thing I'd always dreaded just happened? The atmosphere in the room was charged.

Illumination from a digital clock on the night stand registered the time at half-past one. The muffled drone of my husband's voice, soft but urgent, filtered past my ear as he sat, stiff and rigid, on the side of the bed. So this was the reason for my premature stirring.

Instinctively I bolted upright and watched the color drain from his face as reflected in the moonlight. The jarring jingle of the phone and his uneasy manner then triggered an indigestible fear that plunged me headlong into an unbelievable sequence of terrorizing events.

In a gesture of compassion, Kyle reached over, patted me on the shoulder, and handed me the phone. Frightened, shaken, and confused, I grabbed the piece as unbelievable fear played havoc with my senses.

"Mom...Mom." The sound of my daughter's strangled voice pierced my heart and my mind went instantly limp.

"Matt...Matthew's dead." Her words were raw.

"What?" The beat of my heart instantly accelerated. I thought it would explode.

Still Haley's message continued; her congested sobs and staggered hiccups ripping my heart to shreds. "He's dead—killed in a car crash—his car—by himself—the

1

hospital—ambulance..."

The silence in the room was deafening.

"Mom... Mom...Hello?"

"I...I don't believe it." My words were stammered, but my mind froze. And although her words continued, my heart refused to understand what my ears were hearing.

Terrorized, I grappled at her words. What had she just said? Matthew's dead? I couldn't comprehend her words. Matthew's dead...Matthew's dead. Thoughts of horror and unimaginable fear again surfaced as her words tumbled over and over in my head.

Still in a daze, I drew a sharp breath as gut wrenching terror again swept through me. A bolt of lightning could not have been more damaging. Now overwrought and crazed, I began to spiral downward into an insidious pit of horror. Would I ever climb out of the abyss I'd just fallen into?

Then, in unrecognizable detachment, and little by little, the unspeakable details of my twenty-two year old son's last moments began to emerge.

Shortly after eleven o'clock Tuesday evening the disastrous evening began. After driving to the home of his cousin following his second-shift job, Matthew made a fatal decision. Desiring a fast meal to satisfy his hunger, he decided a quick trip to Taco Bell would be short, and simple.

His foot heavy on the petal, he sped down an unfamiliar road amid a torrential downpour of rain. Oblivious to a sharp curve ahead the locals had dubbed *Dead Man's Curve*, he continued his short trek at breakneck speed. Then, as his car slid into the long-famed curve, it hydroplaned on the slick water-drenched pavement, and spun out of control.

But overcorrecting his mistake only triggered the car to flip several times on its way down a steep embankment. The now compacted auto promptly slammed into a huge tree, preventing its further descent into the ravine. Later his car would be documented as a total loss.

However, due to the nature of the accident, Matt's

head was knocked about, and began to swell. Broken ribs, shattered bones, and other injuries were also sustained; and yet he was still alive. But following a fast ride with paramedics to the hospital, his race with life was over.

The police were astonished when they learned he didn't survive his trauma, as they recalled conversing with him while medics loaded him into an ambulance. Reports later indicated the severity of the crash had caused more internal than external injury.

Matt was living with his deceased father's relatives over one-hundred miles from where his step-father Kyle and I lived when the accident occurred. However, for that reason and others, Ashley, his aunt, called my daughter instead of me when she learned of his death. But following the accident, unresolved issues of the past became unimportant and superficial.

Still struggling to comprehend the magnitude of what I'd just heard, I staggered from bed in a stupor. *What could I do? What did I need to do? What did I have to do?*

Life as it was would never be the same again.

The local newspaper reported this story about the accident.

"A man was killed Tuesday night when he lost control of his car and hit some trees at 11:20 p.m.," a spokesperson from the N.C. State Highway Patrol reported.

A 22 year-old man was driving South on U.S. 220 Business when he lost control of a 2001 Chevrolet as he come out of a left curve. "He ran off the right shoulder of the road, overcorrected, and slid around to the left, and went off the shoulder again," said Holcombe.

The car rolled down a steep embankment, where its driver's side hit a tree. The car spun—the passenger's side striking another tree. The driver was transported to a local hospital where he later died.

One rescue squad member at the scene said, "He was conscious and alert and talking to us. He complained of pain in his left arm and left hand." He said later he was surprised to hear of Matt's death.

Trooper G.S. Grissom said the man was not wearing a seat belt and estimated that he was driving 70 in a 55 mph speed limit. Police and fire departments also responded to the call.

Estrangement from Jeremy, my first husband, and his family following our divorce years earlier, and later his death, had caused a rift between the two families. But unusual situations carve out unexpected pathways to again bring people together.

Immediately a call was placed to Ashley, my former sister-in-law, as details and confirmation were essential. But she was as hysterical as my daughter had been, reaching out to me as I was to her. Issues of the past then dissolved as the present crisis claimed prominence.

The details of that horrific evening were later pieced together with information obtained from police, medical personnel, family members, and another former sister-in-law who works as head nurse in an emergency room. Her experience includes first-hand knowledge of catastrophic injuries similar to Matthew's. After the accident she explained in detail how his body had reacted to the accident; and the verity that similar collisions almost always result in instant death. Yet somehow he wasn't killed at the moment of impact, but later passed away in the hospital.

We also learned that his crash had gone undetected for some time as the hour was late and the weather harsh. According to police records, he tried to escape his encapsulated prison, but was unsuccessful. It was also reported that he carried a handgun for protection. Although injured, he was able to drag the weapon from its hiding place and direct a bullet through the already smashed car window, drawing attention to his plight. A couple of police officers were soon on the scene. One was another cousin.

"We'll get you out buddy," Luke said. "Don't worry. You'll make it. We've called an ambulance."

The jaws of life were then employed as medics

rushed to salvage Matthew from his smashed, crushed, and destroyed vehicle. He was then rushed to the hospital complaining of excruciating pain in arm and chest.

The ambulance was in transit as his re-acquainted relatives were alerted, and warned that time was short. They were then instructed to get to the hospital as soon as possible.

Although his head was swelling, most of Matt's injuries were internal as later documented. It was also reported, had he survived, he would most likely have had brain damage. But it wasn't until his heart stopped beating that the hospital staff began to grasp the severity of his injuries. CPR resuscitation was then initiated, but to no avail. He had been in a fast race with death, and death had won.

Did he realize he was taking his final breath? I do not know. What I do understand is that God granted him a few extra minutes to make his peace. Did he? Eternity alone holds the key.

But the excruciating pain he reported to paramedics was possibly due to broken bones or shattered bone fragments probing the heart cavity. One report indicated his heart may have been pierced with a shard of broken rib, causing a fast and brutal demise.

Family members failed to arrive in time to see him before he died, a short time after his arrival to the emergency room. Police records later indicated no alcohol or drugs were found in his body. An autopsy was then suggested, but what was the point. Matthew was dead. Nothing would ever change that fact.

In Memory

Born May 10, 1982 ~ Died July 28, 2004

It's been a day of sadness
On my journey into grief
Sometimes my tears would fall like rain
Yet promised no relief

It's been a year of sadness
Of brokenness and fears
Sometimes my mind became dead numb
Engulfed by floods of tears

But God has been so very close
His Spirit hovered near
His promises are true
So what had I to fear?

He promised me my children
Together would be there
At that dinner in the sky
That Jesus will prepare

God the Father had to grieve
When His son had to die
So I could have a hope
To see my son on high

On this journey into grief
My sorrow's just a part
For memories of the past
I hold within my heart

Yet looking to the future
Is my hope and gain

DEATH CAME QUICKLY

For soon the sun will shine again
And push away the rain

And with his shy but silly grin
My son again I'll see
Then together with those we love
We'll spend eternity

By faith I know God's word is true
On my journey into grief
A time to weep, a time to mourn
And then He gives sweet peace

© *J. Hannah Lloyd*

Chapter Two

Death

The Bible refers to death as sleep; or being asleep. "...When I awake, I am still with you" (*Psalms 139:18*)

Death (deth)—noun

The act of dying; the end of life; the total and permanent cessation of all the vital functions of an organism. The state of being dead: to lie still in death.

—Synonyms
1. Decease, demise, passing, departure

—Antonyms
1. Birth, life.

"Give light to my eyes, or I will sleep in death..." (*Psalms 13: 3*)
   "Multitudes who sleep in the dust of the earth will awake: some to everlasting life, others to shame and everlasting contempt (*Daniel 2: 2*)
   "We will not all sleep, but we will all be changed—in a flash, in the twinkling of an eye, at the last trumpet. (*1 Corinthians 15:51*)
   "I would be asleep and at rest..." (*Job 3:13*)
   "He went in and said to them, "Why all this commotion and wailing? The child is not dead but asleep" (*Mark 5:39*)
   "For when David had served God's purpose in his

own generation, he fell asleep; he was buried with his fathers..." (*Acts 13:36*)

"But Christ has indeed been raised from the dead, the first fruits of those who have fallen asleep. For since death came through a man, the resurrection of the dead comes also through a man.

For as in Adam all die, so in Christ all will be made alive. But each in his own turn: Christ, the first fruits; then, when he comes, those who belong to him.

Then the end will come, when he hands over the kingdom to God the Father after he has destroyed all dominion, authority and power. For he must reign until he has put all his enemies under his feet. The last enemy to be destroyed is death" (*1 Corinthians 15: 20-26*)

"Brothers, we do not want you to be ignorant about those who fall asleep, or to grieve like the rest of men, who have no hope. We believe that Jesus died and rose again and so we believe that God will bring with Jesus those who have fallen asleep in him. According to the Lord's own word, we tell you that we who are still alive, who are left till the coming of the Lord, will certainly not precede those who have fallen asleep" (*2 Thessalonians 4: 13-15*)

***

Losing a close friend or relative in death could be the most devastating occurrence one will ever experience. The emotion of loss, the devastation of emptiness, and constant waves of draining hopelessness will be overwhelming, and could quickly overtake a conscious mind. Unrelenting sorrow will then rip into the core of everything one has always believed. Disparaging thoughts can even question the existence of God.

But the rawness of grief won't be defined in mere words. These harsh feelings are unlike anything ever before experienced. They will strip all innocence from life, and zap a person's very strength with a feeling so staggering the Bible discloses this truth in two simple words. "Jesus wept" (*John 11:35*).

Although his words may seem trivial, the emotional pain he felt must have been overwhelming.

The Story of Lazarus

Jesus, our perfect example, revealed his own grief by shedding tears of sorrow when his friend Lazarus died. And, for the rest of us, there's no way around the grieving process. Without option or delay, complicated or not; when sorrow presents itself, we will go through pain and sorrow. There is no other choice.

"Now a man named Lazarus was sick. He was from Bethany, the village of Mary and her sister Martha. This Mary, whose brother Lazarus now lay sick, was the same one who poured perfume on the Lord and wiped his feet with her hair. So the sisters sent word to Jesus, "Lord, the one you love is sick."

When he heard this, Jesus said, "This sickness will not end in death. No, it is for God's glory so that God's Son may be glorified through it."

Jesus loved Martha and her sister and Lazarus. Yet when he heard that Lazarus was sick, he stayed where he was two more days. Then he said to his disciples, "Let us go back to Judea."

"But Rabbi," they said, "a short while ago the Jews tried to stone you, and yet you are going back there?"

Jesus answered, "Are there not twelve hours of daylight? A man who walks by day will not stumble, for he sees by this world's light. It is when he walks by night that he stumbles, for he has no light."

After he had said this, he went on to tell them, "Our friend Lazarus has fallen asleep; but I am going there to wake him up."

His disciples replied, "Lord, if he sleeps, he will get better."

Jesus had been speaking of his death, but his disciples thought he meant natural sleep. So then he told them plainly, "Lazarus is dead, and for your sake I am glad I was not there, so that you may believe. But let us go to him."

Then Thomas (called Didymus) said to the rest of the disciples, "Let us also go, that we may die with him."

On his arrival, Jesus found that Lazarus had already been in the tomb for four days. Bethany was less than two miles from Jerusalem and many Jews had come to Martha and Mary to comfort them in the loss of their brother.

When Martha heard that Jesus was coming, she went out to meet him, but Mary stayed at home. "Lord," Martha said to Jesus, "if you had been here, my brother would not have died. But I know that even now God will give you whatever you ask."

Jesus said to her, "Your brother will rise again."

Martha answered, "I know he will rise again in the resurrection at the last day."

Jesus said to her, "I am the resurrection and the life. He who believes in me will live, even though he dies; and whoever lives and believes in me will never die. Do you believe this?"

"Yes, Lord," she told him, "I believe that you are the Christ, the Son of God, who was to come into the world."

And after she had said this, she went back and called her sister Mary aside. "The Teacher is here," she said, "and is asking for you."

When Mary heard this, she got up quickly and went to him.

Now Jesus had not yet entered the village, but was still at the place where Martha had met him. When the Jews who had been with Mary in the house, comforting her, noticed how quickly she got up and went out, they followed her, supposing she was going to the tomb to mourn there.

When Mary reached the place where Jesus was and saw him, she fell at his feet and said, "Lord, if you had been here, my brother would not have died."

When Jesus saw her weeping, and the Jews who had come along with her also weeping, he was deeply moved in

spirit and troubled. "Where have you laid him?" he asked.
"Come and see, Lord," they replied.

Jesus wept.

Then the Jews said, "See how he loved him!

But some of them said, "Could not he who opened the eyes of the blind man have kept this man from dying?"

Jesus, once more deeply moved, came to the tomb. It was a cave with a stone laid across the entrance.

"Take away the stone," he said.

"But, Lord," said Martha, the sister of the dead man, "by this time there is a bad odor, for he has been there four days."

Then Jesus said, "Did I not tell you that if you believed, you would see the glory of God?"

So they took away the stone. Then Jesus looked up and said, "Father, I thank you that you have heard me. I knew that you always hear me, but I said this for the benefit of the people standing here, that they may believe that you sent me.

When he had said this, Jesus called in a loud voice, "Lazarus, come out!"

The dead man came out, his hands and feet wrapped with strips of linen, and a cloth around his face.

Jesus said to them, "Take off the grave clothes and let him go" (*John 11:1-44*)

Chapter Three

Confronting Death

One way I learned to cope following the death of my son was to write poetry. When feelings were raw, I scribbled them down. When memories flooded my soul, I put them in writing. And when despair was my only focus, God placed words of prose into my spirit, and I transferred them all to paper.

Then, as time moved forward, so did my desire to journal my thoughts and feelings. Poetry then became a memorial of grief—a channel of hope to mend my troubled heart; as losing my baby was a horrible finale to all accumulated hopes and dreams.

Music of consolation played over and over again became therapeutic as my need for confirmation, assurance, and consolation was essential. Songs by Cheryl Salem, a well-known Christian vocalist who lost her daughter Gabrielle to cancer, was another anchor in my storm. Her music also re-affirmed my confidence in God, as I realized she too understood the harshness of death.

The staggering newness of a loss will be overwhelming. Yet Christian music has a way of softening the rush of insanity that tends to flood the mind. Christian material on grief can also be consoling as well as informative. A recorded message from the Bible will also provide needed comfort, support, and consolation.

Realize that after a loved one dies, finding ways to manage new bouts of sorrow and feelings of insecurity is essential as raw insanity and gripping emotion will surely claim every waking moment if allowed.

A new hobby could be another way of releasing sorrow in a positive way. Your creative side will then emerge, and bring new seasons of hope to your shattered soul. Activities such as writing, gardening, painting, or volunteering are also avenues that help bring healing and restoration to body, mind, and spirit.

New interests can also activate a new sense of self-worth and value. Finding fresh outlets of focus will help to lessen the amount of time needed to recover from your trauma of grief. Perhaps starting a grief ministry of your own will bring the emotional healing you need, and desire.

Grieving

"The Lord is gracious and righteous; our God is full of compassion" (*Psalms 116:5*)

Dictionary: Grief - keen mental suffering or distress over affliction or loss; sharp sorrow; painful regret
A cause or occasion of keen distress or sorrow

Synonyms: anguish, heartache, woe, misery; sadness, melancholy, moroseness.

Antonyms: joy.

At an unscheduled and unpredictable moment death will come to call. Like an unexpected visitor, this disruption will one day confront and confuse your very existence. But when it arrives, deep sorrow, unbelievable anguish, and excruciating misery will overtake you as a thief in the night.

"...for you know very well that the day of the Lord will come like a thief in the night" (*I Thessalonians 5:2*)

Death affects everyone in one way or another. It is no stranger. But when I ponder the military, our Heroes, losing their lives on foreign soil far from home, I shudder for their families. Although war has been re-occurring for our great country throughout history, Americans continue to grieve their losses. Each generation has now surrendered countless soldiers to battleground conflicts, or war related deaths, and the number continues to soar.

There's also a combat zone on domestic soil as children are dying far too young. Drugs, alcohol, abuse, and neglect are rampant, and unashamedly steal the lives of our youth. Even the safety of the unborn is in jeopardy as thousands are murdered on any given day in abortion mills. Yet this is made possible as the immoral believe we live in a disposable society.

The parents of a child who has been abducted also aren't immune. Insane uncertainty, without a doubt, then overtakes the mind as questions concerning the very existence and whereabouts of their missing child takes over. All understanding will die as parents, in anguished turmoil, contemplate the unknown—is their child dead or alive?

There are also those who've lost loved ones to violence and murder, and suffer deep sorrow; yet their torment remains hidden. And, in every direction, insidious, insane predators in every walk of life kidnap, rape, and murder our children, or other family members, without any sense of decency or morality; allowing their lust to sacrifice the lives of the innocent.

Satan is evil, and causes men to do wicked things. Then lacking restraint, the immoral accept his vile devices without conscience or concern. Evidence of Satan's malevolence will continue until the end of time.

Storm

Dark storm clouds gather thick
As harsh winds whip about
The brightest light in life
Has died and flickered out

Death's storm will never end
Its harsh winds won't subside
Dark clouds are always near
As memories collide

For 'tho the time will pass
'Mid flash of sun and night
Rain drops its glistening tears
In memory of the light

© J. Hannah Lloyd
2007 Award winning poem

Chapter Four

Stages of Grief

Several stages of sorrow are experienced following the death of a loved one. Although levels of mourning will differ from person to person, the fundamental stages are normal, and documented. However, knowing what to expect while going through the grieving process could be beneficial.

Five basic steps are listed below.

- Denial: Shock and disbelief are the initial feelings that follow the death of a loved one. You will also feel numb and unable to believe this death is real. This stage may last a short time, or an extended period of time. Hours and days will then run together as the mind tries to process the facts of what has happened. This disbelief will also overwhelm as you struggle through this stage.

- Anger: You may become enraged and have trouble sleeping; or be unable to function at a normal pace during this stage. Anger at your loved one can also surface, or anger be expressed in negative ways toward others. This is also the time when grief becomes severe. Strong disbelief that the deceased has gone away can be overwhelming, and cause uncontrollable rage. Although your anger may be kept in check, you will still experience irritation or resentment—either out loud, or in silence.

- Regret: During this stage extreme remorse will surface at not having been more tolerant or understanding of your loved one before they died. Yet this is a normal reaction if there are regrets of any nature. But realizing your inability to apologize, or change the past, may cause emotional distress. However, this is something only time can heal. You may also feel guilt for a variety of reasons.

- Depression: In this stage you will become despondent and lose interest in activities, work, or life in general as emotions are sorted through following a loss. Sudden bouts of crying, or withdraw from others is also normal. It may also be difficult to forgive yourself, but for many reasons. You can even harbor regret that your loved one didn't live a long life. Then feeling out of control could cause depression. But if sadness is overwhelming, medical treatment may be needed for assistance through this stage.

- The final stage of grieving comes when one realizes their loved one has died, is now buried, and no more on this earth. It is what it is. There are no u-turns or reversals in this trauma. As sad as it may be, nothing more can be done to change your circumstance. Now is the time to realize you have your own life to live. As difficult as that may be, try to accept your loved one's death as part of the cycle of life.

It's Over

Tragedy not averted
But hit head on
Life as it was
Is over and done

Last words have been said
Last things have been done
That sad day is now
I buried my son

© *J. Hannah Lloyd*

There's never a set time to complete the basic stages of heartache. It's individually based and depends on one's own ability to cope. But realize, only time can heal a broken heart. And only God can provide the comfort that's needed to heal.

"My heart is broken within me; all my bones tremble" (*Jeremiah 23: 9*)
"...a broken and contrite heart, O God, you will not despise" (*Psalms 51: 17*)

Denial

"Then Jesus said to his disciples, "If anyone would come after me, he must **deny** himself and take up his cross and follow me" (*Matthew 16:24*)

Definition of *denial*—an assertion that something said, believed, alleged, etc., is false; a disbelief in the existence or reality of a thing. The refusal to recognize or acknowledge; a disowning or disavowal: *Peter's denial of Christ.*

Psychology: an unconscious defense mechanism used to reduce anxiety by denying thoughts, feelings, or facts that are consciously intolerable.

Synonyms: disavowal, disclaimer, repudiation.

Antonyms: admission, acknowledgment, confession

Broke

Death broke my heart
Like daggers and splinters
With sharp, shattered edges
And raw broken ridges

Death broke my heart
Exploded like a coke
With shards of broken glass
And yes, it is still broke

© *J. Hannah Lloyd*

Oh the memories of happier times when everything seemed right in the world, and sadness was as far away as China. But when death came to call, it was easier to pretend the certainty of mortality didn't exist than to accept the truth of humanity.

How could someone so active die so fast, and my dreams turn into nightmares?

Denial is more than a six letter word. But the ability to accept the death of a loved one is a rejection of unprecedented response, and difficult to comprehend. However, an unexpected or sudden death will cause even more emotional shock following the news.

Some will try to forget what lies ahead, or ignore their reality while hoping the situation will go away. But this denial could cause serious problems. Therapy may then be required in order to confront and overcome the rejection of a loved one's death. However, if this is the case, denial is an obstacle that needs to be addressed before one can move ahead with life in general.

Anger

...for man's **anger** does not bring about the righteous life that God desires. *(James 1:20)*

Definition of *anger*: a strong feeling of displeasure and belligerence aroused by a wrong; wrath; ire. Or anguish— wrath.

Synonyms:

1. To feel resentment, exasperation; ANGER, FURY, INDIGNATION, RAGE deep and strong feelings aroused by injury, injustice, wrong, etc. ANGER is the general term for a sudden violent displeasure: *a burst of anger.* INDIGNATION implies deep and justified anger: *indignation at cruelty or against corruption.* RAGE is vehement anger: *rage at being frustrated.* FURY is rage so great that it resembles insanity.

2. To displease, vex, irritate, exasperate, infuriate, enrage, incense, madden.

But in order to survive your trauma, let God be the shoulder you lean upon.

Regret

"Godly sorrow brings repentance that leads to salvation and leaves no **regret**, but worldly sorrow brings death" (*II Corinthians 7:10*)

Definition of *regret*: to feel sorrow or remorse for (an act, fault, disappointment, etc.): *He no sooner spoke than he regretted it.*

To think of with a sense of loss: *to regret one's vanished youth*. A sense of loss, disappointment, dissatisfaction, etc. a feeling of sorrow or remorse for a fault, act, loss, disappointment, and so on.

Synonyms:

1. to deplore, lament, bewail, bemoan, mourn, sorrow, and grieve. REGRET, PENITENCE, REMORSE— To imply a sense of sorrow about events in the past, usual wrongs committed or errors made. REGRET is distress of mind, sorrow for what has been done or failed to be done: *to have no regrets.*

PENITENCE implies a sense of sin or misdoing, a feeling of contrition and determination not to sin again: *a humble sense of penitence.* REMORSE implies pangs, qualms of conscience, a sense of guilt, regret, and repentance for sins committed, wrongs done, or duty not performed: *a deep sense of remorse.*

Antonyms:

1. Rejoice.
2. Joy.

***

Depression

"This can be nothing but **sadness** of heart" (*Nehemiah 2:2*)

Definition of *Depression*: a sunken place or part.

Psychiatry: a condition of general emotional dejection and withdrawal; sadness greater and more prolonged than that warranted by any objective reason. Sadness; gloom; dejection, dullness.

1. Synonyms: discouragement, despondency.

To grieve for a long period of time is not recommended. Depression may then set in, and lead to serious medical and mental issues. Learn to forgive yourself, and don't allow emotions of regret to take over. Visit a doctor if you later become unable to cope with the stress of heartache. It may also be helpful to join a grief recovery group nearby. Sharing like stories and similarities with others who are also grieving has its own restorative benefits. Connecting with other grief survivors on the Internet could also be another way of coping with your loss.

Grieving

My son, my son
My youngest one
One year ago passed away

But grief remains
A sad refrain
For each new day

© *J. Hannah Lloyd*

Acceptance

Jesus replied, "Not everyone can **accept** this word, but only those to whom it has been give" (*Matthew 19:11*)
"Even in laughter the heart may ache, and joy may **end** in grief" (*Proverbs 14:13*)

Definition of *Acceptance*: The process of accepting, the act of taking or receiving something offered. The act of believing approval, belief in something, agreement

Will I ever be able to accept the death of a loved one? The most understandable answer is "No." But with God's help and the healing of time, much of the bitterness caused by this death should diminish.

However, in the process of relinquishing your grief, try to remember all the positive accomplishments of the deceased, and recall optimistic and joyful moments spent together. Push aside thoughts that cause hurt and pain, and concentrate on memories that bring laughter and joy. For by re-directing our thoughts, the constant ache of a broken heart should begin to diminish. After that, more positive recollections could become your fondest memories. In fact, these are the treasures that won't fade with the passing of time.

When death strikes and questions arise that require answers one doesn't have, it's best not to dwell on those uncertainties. Learn to embrace your joyful memories and leave the rest in God's hands. Try to remember the best of times, and don't concern yourself with the unknown as you move forward through the grieving process. Then retain all unsurpassed reminiscences deep within the heart, and leave the rest in God's hands.

One special memory shared by Matthew's aunt was when she saw him in church as he stood with head bowed and eyes closed. This was just days before his death.

"For if their rejection is their reconciliation of the world, what will their acceptance be but **life from the**

dead?" (*Romans 11:15*)

"Believe in the Lord Jesus, and you will be saved—you and your household" (*Acts 16:31*)

But everywhere I'm looking for him—in the faces of young men in places he would go. Will I see him at a music store strumming a model guitar? Or will I glimpse him as he boards a crowded elevator? Could he now be the lead guitarist in his own band?

Although thoughts of what could have been will surface, learn to direct the negative to happier times, and concentrate on them. Be positive as you sort through your memories. Lay aside disappointment and regret, and realize that your loved one would want you to enjoy the rest of your life without the burden of regret resting on your shoulders.

I Think of Him

When winter blows
In drifts of snow
I think of him,
His eyes aglow

And all the young girls
That I meet
He could be kissing
In the street

He would have grown
To six feet tall
With friends he'd loafer
At the mall

He'd be a star
In his own band
A favorite guitar
In his hand

Oh how I yearn
To hear him say
"I love you Mom.
I'm back to stay."

© *J. Hannah Lloyd*

"There is no fear in love. Perfect love drives out fear, because fear has to do with punishment. The one who fears is not made perfect in love" (*John 4:18*)

Perhaps it's difficult to revisit places that allow memories of the past to surface regarding your loved one. But if this is the case, try to protect yourself, for a time, from that distress. Choose *not* to visit those places until ready to confront and lay aside your emotions of sorrow.

Grief has no guidelines to surrender to. Feelings of sadness will come and go at will, without boundaries to thwart the inevitable. Your sorrow may be long in duration, but God will restore with joy and give you peace, if allowed.

"Weeping may endure for a night but joy comes in the morning" (*Psalms 30:5) (KJV)*

Everyone going through grief cannot function at 100 percent capacity the initial days and months following the death of a loved one. Patience and understanding are needed during this period of time. Accept assistance when offered, and allow yourself time to recover from the trauma of your loss. It's your time to grieve. Use this time wisely as you transition from sorrow into acceptance during this stage of grief.

It's also important to refrain from making key decisions during this time. If possible, wait at least one year following the death of a loved one as issues associated with grieving could cloud good judgment

"...Now is your time of grief, but I will see you again and you will rejoice, and no one will take away your joy" (*John 16:22*)

"I tell you the truth, you will weep and mourn.... You will grieve, but your grief will turn to joy" (*John 16:20*)

"...the month when their sorrow was turned into joy and their mourning into a day of celebration" (*Esther 9:22*)

Chapter Five

Why me?

You may ask, "Why me? How did this happen to me? Why am I the one who has to grieve at this time in my life?"

But, why not you? The Bible explains that God is no respecter of persons. "For God does not show favoritism" (*Romans 2:11*)

"He causes his sun to rise on the evil and the good, and sends rain on the righteous and the unrighteous" (*Matthew 5:45*)

We don't know why things happen the way they do. In fact, we may even feel responsible for the demise of a loved one, or blame God for their untimely death. Still it's important to realize that God is in control even though we may have lost ours. His promise to be with us during our struggles is our only hope and strength. (Psalms 46:3)

Although you may feel alone in your sorrow, if you allow those around you to provide assistance, your anguish will be easier to manage.

There are also many resources available that will benefit beyond your initial sorrow. But remember. God is our complete source of strength. His word, the Bible, will provide all that's needed for comfort and healing of heart, mind, and soul. Friends and loved ones will fill in the gap as we sort through the maze of grief.

***

Sorrow

It's a hurt
That won't go away
It was here yesterday
And it's here today

It won't be gone
Even after tomorrow
It has its grip
It is called sorrow

This painful hurt
Is here to stay
Long is the night
And long is the day

I can't go forward
In sorrow and pain
The sun never shines
There's always more rain

© *J. Hannah Lloyd*

Visiting the cemetery often brings a sense of re-connection for family and friends. For others it will be a painful reminder that their loved one has died. But this all depends on the relationship shared with the deceased.

Placing memorials and flowers at the gravesite can also bring a sense of closure while demonstrating love for a deceased loved one, and others who are left to grieve. Many times flowers and a memorial cross remain on the roadside where an accident claimed a life. Sadness may then overwhelm when viewing these special mementos, if but for a moment.

But in order to process your emotions, allow those feelings to surface from time to time as they are beneficial for emotional restoration. And, over time, your sentiments may bring a sense of acceptance and closure to your heart.

Chapter Six

How to Grieve

There's never a wrong or right way to mourn. The actions of the sorrowful depend solely on the individual. Lamenting may be private or collective. Grieving may be loud or hushed. But through it all, realize you're not alone.

Grief has no boundaries to claim. It will occur at unexpected moments in unexpected forms of anguish, but may become critical if one feels abandoned, and alone.

Wrenching sobs that leave one gasping for air will also occur. Emotions of anguish that burn into the very depths of your soul will again surface, and leave nothing but charred ashes and ruin. Writhing sensations of grief that have no measure will then charge in, and greet you before you're fully awake in the morning. Unprocessed emotions will also tug at your insides until it feels you're going to burst. Tears will then gush forth, but at unexpected moments.

But out-of-control torrents that leave one reeling in spasms of sorrow need to be addressed. Open wounds of grief are easy to penetrate, and will deplete your very strength if left unrestrained.

There is no clear path to healing from grief and sorrow. It will take time, even years of time, to sort through the depths of heartache. But as you sort through the maze, allow the Holy Spirit to give you the comfort you need for restoration and renewal.

***

I Am Not Whole

I am not whole
I feel so weak
I'm grieving for
Life incomplete

A hurt so deep
To feel such shame
At all the struggle
Without the gain

Mistakes were made
But can't atone
A weight that's borne
On me alone

My life feels spent
I tried so hard
To fill the gap
But it's been marred

When waiting for
New change ahead
Your death then caused
Deep sorrow instead

© *J. Hannah Lloyd*

Chapter Seven

Bible History on Grieving

The Israelites knew how to grieve. They were the experts.

Sackcloth was worn on the body and ashes placed on the head while mourning a death, or grieving a sinful choice they had made. Sackcloth and ashes was the garment of mourning, and a witness to others that grieving was underway, and in full process.

The mourners would then walk the street wearing sackcloth and ashes, or sit among the residue outside the gate of the city. This ritual would last thirty days, the designated time of sorrow. During this period they could wallow in their sorrow. But after the rite was completed, the grievers would cleanse themselves, left their anguish behind, and continue to live their lives.

Although the rituals of mourning in today's society are quite different than the era of Bible days, the internal hurt remains the same.

Examples given in the Bible on how to mourn represent an overall way to grieve. In fact, the word of God gives us permission to lament. Many examples of being sorrowful are found throughout the pages of the Bible, and give a historical account of the grieving process. The Israelites, our best exemplar, had many reasons to grieve. Although traditions of the past have ended, we can still learn from them.

After the initial shock of losing a loved one has subsided and a selected amount of time has passed, try to pick up the pieces of your life and again begin to exist.

Because when we allow God to heal our hurts, that remedial will complete the process.

The Bible on How to Mourn

"When Mordecai learned of all that had been done, he tore his clothes, put on **sackcloth** and **ashes**, and went out into the city, wailing loudly and bitterly" (*Esther 4:1*)

"O my people, put on **sackcloth** and roll in **ashes**; mourn with bitter wailing as for an only son, for suddenly the destroyer will come upon us" (*Jeremiah 6:26*)

"Then Jacob tore his clothes, put on **sackcloth** and mourned for his son many days. All his sons and daughters came to comfort him, but he refused to be comforted. "No," he said, "in mourning will I go down to the grave to my son." So his father wept for him" (*Genesis 37:34*)

"Then David said to Joab and all the people with him, "Tear your clothes and put on **sackcloth** and walk in mourning in front of Abner." King David himself walked behind the bier.

They buried Abner in Hebron, and the king wept aloud at Abner's tomb. All the people wept also" (*2 Samuel 3:31*)

"In the streets they wear **sackcloth**; on the roofs and in the public squares they all wail, prostrate with weeping" (*Isaiah 15:3*)

"So put on **sackcloth**, lament and wail..." (*Jeremiah 4:8*)

"The elders of the Daughter of Zion sit on the ground in silence; they have sprinkled **dust** on their heads and put on **sackcloth**. The young women of Jerusalem have bowed their heads to the ground. My eyes fail from weeping, I am in torment within, my heart is poured out on the ground ..." (*Lamentations 2:10, 11*)

"They will shave their heads because of you and will put on **sackcloth**. They will weep over you with anguish of soul and with bitter mourning" (*Ezekiel 27:31*)

I will turn your religious feasts into mourning and all you're singing into weeping. I will make all of you wear **sackcloth** and shave your heads. I will make that time like mourning for an only son and the end of it like a bitter day" (*Amos 8:10*)

A Season of my Life

July twenty-eight my youngest son
In a car crash lost his life
At the age of twenty-two
My heart was stabbed with a knife

What will I do? What will I say?
How will I react on a normal day?
Will the pain recede and lose its grip
Or will it never go away?

My heart-it aches—it burns and tears
The pain is so severe
My eyes, so red—the tears won't stop
My mind so full, and will not clear

Although I know God's in control
As I lay down for the night
In my heart I'll always know
Things will never be quite right

© *J. Hannah Lloyd*

Quiet moments may bring some relief as memories of good times again surface. But following those reminders will be the reality of death as the truth of it closes in around you. Even though it's evident a loved one has died, the most sensitive may not truly realize you're still sorrowful as you've learned the secret of how to grieve in silence. Later, in the aftermath, anything can trigger sorrow and grief. Even a song will even trigger a session of sorrow and tears, or a memory bring you to your knees.

Actions and events once enjoyed no longer bring happiness. Holidays and joyful seasons are also dreaded, feel strange, or unseasonably sad.

Although memories of fun times may surface, the dreadful truth of why things are different will suddenly grab you by the throat, and wrap around your mind. Then, in an instant, you're again back in that dreaded cycle of grief. This sequence of mourning has now become your reality.

Did you know?

Did you know?
And that they say
Your heart can break
And fall away?

Your heart can fracture
Be crushed and split
Can also be damaged
No longer be fit

My heart is now broken
By a life that was hard
My son is now dead
My heart now a shard

My soul is in pieces
And shattered it seems
Since my son's cruel death
All hopes are just dreams

This truth has now come
And my heart is not well
It's fractured and crushed
Yet others can't tell

© *J. Hannah Lloyd*

Listed below are suggestions that should help minimize the hurt of sorrow during the stages of grief.

- Talk about your loved one on a regular basis

- Mention them by name, and in conversation daily

- If you're sad, say so

- Don't hide your feelings

- If you need extra help, don't be afraid to ask

- Journaling is a great way to express your feelings

- Continue positive routines each day. Be sure to exercise and eat right to maintain your own health and well-being

- Join a grief-recovery or grief-support group

- Continue to pray for God's comfort and assistance

- Don't be afraid to ask others to pray for you

Grieving God's Way, a book written by Margaret Brownley, indicates it may take as long as five years to work through the heartache of losing a loved one. For others it will be longer.

As a footnote, don't try to rush the grieving process. Only time can heal a broken heart. And only God can repair a damaged soul.

Broken Heart

I just miss you
Oh, so much
Life keeps moving
In such a rush

People passing by
But they don't know
My heart is broken
And healing slow

© *J. Hannah Lloyd*

Chapter Eight

Emotions of Fear

It's imperative that a proper amount of time be put aside to grieve, and permission given to lament. Then, if allowed, the act of mourning and seasons of sorrow will later bring healing and resolution. And although your tunnel of sorrow may be long in duration, joy will come in the morning.

"Weeping may endure for a night but joy comes in the morning" (*Psalms 30:5*) *(KJV)*

Fear is an emotion that often emerges following the death of a loved one. You may be terrified you'll be the next one to die. Or, you may be afraid someone else close to you will pass away in the immediate future.

But panic and dread will be devastating if allowed to overtake the mind. Apprehension of the future may also be upsetting if permitted to continue. Nightmares, terror, and phobias can also surface.

However, it's important to understand that fear is a normal reaction following the death of a loved one, and shouldn't linger too long.

God often reminds us in the Bible not to fear. It's even more important in this season of our life. Allow his word to guide and console as you move forward though the grieving process.

"Fear thou not; for I am with thee: be not dismayed; for I am thy God: I will strengthen thee; yea, I will help thee; yea, I will uphold thee with the right hand of my righteousness" (*Isaiah 41:10*)

***

Never Again

You will always be twenty-two
You will never be old or new
You will never again call and say
"Mom, I'm home again" today

Never again will you laugh or smile
Never again will you stay a while
Never again will you give a hug
Never again will you show your love

No more birthdays will come and go
Life will never be fast or slow
You will never again stay the night
All is dark, and gone is the light

No gifts to give with your name on them
No mail, or cards, or letters from friends
No one will call to talk to you
No bride to you will say 'I do'

There won't be children with your name
You'll never achieve wealth or fame
Holidays without you will have no meaning
Memories about you only come by dreaming

No more vacations with you in mind
No more learning of any kind
No more driving that sporty car
No more traveling from near to far

Your life is over. Your dreams are dead.
All hopes for you are crushed instead
Life without you won't be the same;
And always tears when we mention your name

But I'm so glad I shared your life
For all it was—there still was strife
Though short is was, it still was yours
And for the hurt you left—no cures

© *J. Hannah Lloyd*

"...Whether a tree falls to the south or to the north, in the place where it falls, there will it lie." *(Ecclesiastes 11: 3)*

After death nothing can be altered or changed. It is what it is. Although difficult to accept, it's best to alleviate as much sorrow as possible during the initial hours and days following your loss.

One way is to focus on your loved one's good accomplishments. Recall and appreciate the relationship you shared, and reminiscence over memories that bring laughter and pleasure. Then reclaim those moments and cherish them as personal treasure.

But when a young one dies, it tends to cause more sorrow than is normal, as part of the family legacy has been removed for future generations.

Children that would have been born will never exist. A potential son-in-law or daughter-in-law never will enhance the holiday gatherings. And there will never be grandchildren from this line in the future.

The family tree will never completely flourish with branches and new bouquets of leaves. At least one branch will never again grow, and part of the tree will remain empty and barren. Life is now empty, and hollow. The joy and excitement of a full house has also ceased.

What was normal and routine is now irregular and unusual. And all that remains are memories of the past, and sorrow for what could have been, but never will be.

***

Remember the Good Times

We don't always
Have to be sad
Just remember the good times
That he had

Remember his birthdays
And his birth
Remember the wonder
And count the worth

Remember the swing
In the back yard
Remember ballgames
When he played hard

Remember his laughter
The fun he had
Remember his jokes
When you were sad

Remember excitement
When Christmas time came
His surprise and delight
With that new-fangled game

Remember vacation
With sand, crabs, and ocean
His cool guitar playing
Notes strung with emotion

We don't always
Have to be sad.
Remember the good times
That he had

© *J. Hannah Lloyd*

The best memories of my deceased son are the funny happenings that occurred during his childhood. Although the innocence of youth passed way too soon, many humorous memories continue to bring joy and laughter. Those moments are still delightful to recall, and help to ease our personal pain and sorrow.

Recalling Childhood Antics

Matthew could make the cutest remarks that were, in reality, quite profound. One remains a favorite.

While watching a thunder storm approach, two-year-old Matt, deep in childish wonder, piped up and said, "The thunder claps its hands. The bad clouds pushed the good clouds away." And, it was so.

Years later when our family spent the week-end camping in the Blue Ridge Mountains of Western North Carolina, another memory was created.

Matthew loved playing hard and his clothing was often covered in dirt and mud. But one evening, after a busy day of accumulated grime and muck, he was sent to the bathhouse for a shower; and reminded to wash away the debris he was covered in. Yet predictable Matt had forgotten his towel.

Another camper was waiting outside the bathhouse for his turn in the shower when a clean Matthew emerged. But when asked if the camper saw him naked, he calmly responded. "Oh, no. I had the shampoo bottle between my legs."

And so the memories thrive, and the legacy continues.

Chapter Nine

Emotions of Anger

Anger, a very real emotion, often surfaces following the death of a loved one. But although you may not an angry person by nature, the results of grief often emerge in ways never expected. This strong sensation could then develop in unbelievable ways.

Pondering the death of a loved one may also bring unexpected resentment, or some measure of rage. You may even be annoyed at the one who has died. Or, you could be overly enraged at the situation that caused the death.

A slight irritation, or an abundance of wrath, may also surface when lest expected. Some have even been angry at God, blaming him for their loved one's demise. But in order to move ahead, release the anger, and let God help you overcome your rage.

It's perfectly acceptable to be angry. It's also understandable to want to blame someone, or something, because of your loved one's death. In fact, the Bible gives us permission to be angry. Just be sure your rage is kept in check, and that you don't step out of bounds during this time of sorrow.

"In your anger do not sin. Do not let the sun go down while you are still angry... (Ephesians 4:26)

But if your anger is overwhelming, find someone to talk with that will help you understand your feelings, and can assist in sorting through your rage and sorrow.

***

When You Died

When you were happy
A part of me cheered
And when you were scared
A part of me feared

When you were hurt
A part of me felt pain
And when you were ignored
A part of me felt shame

When you were alone
Then I too felt alone
And when you were angry
A part of me was stone

When you were hungry
A part of me felt empty
And when you were dressed up
A part of me felt lovely

When you were honored
A part of me felt pride
And when you were unhappy
A part of me then cried

But when you died
More than a part of me died

© *J. Hannah Lloyd*

Anger following the death of a loved one can overtake a person in such an overwhelming way it may damage one's ability to remain balanced and coherent. Unexpected sensations of rage can also flood the mind as the facts of your loved one's demise are rationalized.

Memories of the past will then intermingle with the present, causing an inability to function in a rational way. Anxiety and stress may then overwhelm as you struggle through your rage. Resentment and irritation could become your middle name.

Flossie and Freddie

Several years ago I noticed a stray kitten stranded on the side of a busy street; not yet old enough to be on its own. Heavy trucks and large equipment rolled down this road all day long, making existence for a small feline almost impossible. Yet somehow this kitten wasn't killed. And when its hungry cries caught my attention, I crossed the road to rescue it.

But since I was traveling, Flossie became my adopted companion. And when we returned home she joined our growing feline family, and became the favored soul-mate of Freddie, Matthew's personal kitten.

The feline bonding of both kittens was instantaneous, and soon they were inseparable. Both would snuggle in a shared basket under the window. They also ate their food at the same time, and shared their toys. But their bond was a constant reminder of their love for each other. And if one disappeared a short time, the other would cry out until they were reunited. This relationship was unique and special—a love match made in feline heaven.

One year later Flossie disappeared from the home. A distraught Freddie then positioned himself by the door in watchful anticipation of her return; his soulful eyes gazing with sadness into the distance. It was obvious he longed for her as every action reflected his feelings. His soul-mate was gone, and he was confused by the sorrow that consumed him.

Yet missing posters yielded no result. And, over time, Freddie realized Flossie wasn't coming home. He then became reclusive and unresponsive, and his appetite diminished as he continued to grieve for her. But after several weeks of patient waiting, he stopped his surveillance at the door. And he never again bonded with another cat, but became a loner.

However, this was heart-wrenching and difficult to watch; a sad ending to a wonderful attraction. Freddie's demeanor was forever changed, and my heart ached for him. I also grieved over Flossie, missing her as much as Freddie loved her.

Freddie was angry that Flossie was gone. But I was even more saddened when my son died. Yet, in both our hearts, there was a lack of understanding.

Sin and Death

Its best not to accuse God for the death of a loved one, but to understand what ignited this derivation. In fact, Satan is the instigator of all sadness and deception. Because of his trickery, Adam and Eve sinned. And, because of their sin, disease and death were introduced to the world.

"Then the Lord God said to the woman, "What is this you have done?" "The woman said, "The serpent deceived me, and I ate" (*Genesis 3:13*)

"Therefore, just as **sin** entered the world through one man, and **death** through **sin**, in this way **death** came to all men..." (*Romans 5:12*)

"Nevertheless, **death** reigned from the time of Adam to the time of Moses, even over those who did not **sin** by breaking a command, as did Adam, who was a pattern of the one to come" (*Romans 5:14*)

***

Silent Cries

It's hard to see through tears
That veil large, swollen eyes
As anger, pain, and hurt
Gives way to silent cries

© *J. Hannah Lloyd*

You may be annoyed at the timing of a loved one's death. Or, perhaps reconciliation didn't have a chance to take place. Anger could also be aimed at someone else without realizing the reason for your rage.

Resentment may overwhelm, if allowed, because of the way a loved one died. But for the good of yourself, and others, it's best to let the rage go. Try working through your anger without blaming others. Internalized resentments could paralyze emotions on the inside.

But in order to survive your sorrow, let God's word to be your guide as you transition from anger into healing.

Chapter Ten

Emotions of Regret

If a loved one struggled with disease and pain, relief at their passing may be instantaneous. However, it doesn't accomplish anything to experience regret over those feelings.

Try putting your thoughts into perspective, and realize that your loved one is no longer suffering. Also, if a Christian, their desired goal has been realized. Allow that comfort to sustain as you work through your pain and sorrow.

I Remember

Love is strong
When hearts are tender
I think of you
And then remember

Your childhood years
I remember them all
The things you did
When you were small

You loved life well
And as you grew
Everything to you
Was fresh and new

But then you grew to man
While making choices wrong
Your life became a burden,
That crushed your happy song

You lost all you had gained
And had to start anew
But I was nowhere near
To show my love to you

And yet I remember you
My young adventurous one
Your life was not in vain
You were my precious son

© *J. Hannah Lloyd*

If you have regret in any form, learn from your mistakes, and accept what cannot be changed. Then pardon yourself, and let go of all regrets.

A Spark of Personality

Matthew had a unique way of speaking whatever came to mind. His grams often recalled how *adult* he articulated his words, even as a three-year-old.

Matt, toys in hand, once spent a quiet morning with her while she visited a friend. Then, as he played by himself in the room, Grams and her friend chatted nearby. But all of a sudden, Matthew stopped his play, looked Grams squarely in the face, and asked, "Now, what was that you just said?"

She and her friend were astounded at his interest as they had no idea he was listening to their conversation.

The other grandmother remembered an incident while shopping with four-year-old Matthew at the grocery store.

As they shopped, a rather heavyset lady carrying an oversized handbag ambled past and stopped in the bread isle nearby. Matt, hands on hips, stood in silence staring, and then asked, "Do you think your pocketbook's big enough?"

Every spring Matthew and his two siblings Haley and Austin, played little league baseball—but on separate teams. But once the players were assigned a team, their new coach would call to discuss the practice schedule.

One evening the telephone rang, and Matthew skipped over to answer it. But after saying "Hello," a strange look crossed his face. He then asked the caller, "What kind of house are you?" and handed the phone to Austin.

Austin looked puzzled. "Who is it?" he asked.

"It's your baseball coach, Mr. House," Matthew said. But under his breath he mumbled, "What kind of name is *House*?"

***

Memories are all that's left once a loved one has passed. But at this point, feelings of remorse need to be laid to rest.

Now is the time to concentrate on happier moments spent with your loved one, and lay aside depressive thoughts and emotions. But don't allow the past to overtake the future. Place your trust in God, and let him give you solace and comfort as you move beyond your sorrow.

Chapter Eleven

Pit of Despair

Harboring feelings of rage, sorrow, disbelief, regret, and blame are often difficult to overcome. Twisted thoughts, angry spurts, and the desire to condemn others are also normal reactions following the death of a loved one. But at some point, all negative emotions must be relinquished, and put into proper perspective.

Appreciate positive memories, refute negative ones, and move ahead with determination to survive your sorrow. Also refrain from placing blame, even on yourself. Remember your loved one for who they were, and allow an optimistic outlook into your future to surface.

But if one harbors regret, and has difficulty forgiving, relinquish all to God whose unending love and mercy will saturate your soul. Leave the pain in the hands of the One who's more than able to embrace your anguish, and give you peace.

"That is why I am suffering as I am. Yet I am not ashamed, because I know in whom I have believed, and am convinced that **he is able** to guard what I have entrusted to him for that day" (*II Timothy 1:12*)

"Now may the Lord of **peace** himself **give you peace** at all times and in every way" (*2 Thessalonians 3:16*)

***

All That Remains

All that remains
Are broken hearts
Shattered dreams
Unfinished starts

All that remains
Are ashes in an urn?
Buried next a granite marker
Covered by a funeral fern

All that remains
Are lonely visits
Holiday sadness
With graveyard limits

All that remains
As life goes on
Is daily withdrawal
And being alone

All that remains
Is missing you
Day and night
In shades of blue

All that remains
When life is through
Is looking forward
To being with you

© *J. Hannah Lloyd*

Following an unexpected death are feelings of horrific despair. The sudden realization that you're not in control, and powerless to go backward, may cause depressive thoughts and desperate actions. Still it's best to mourn in your own way as you shuffle through the grieving process. But don't be afraid to express your feelings as they may generate some closure to your misery.

In the Pit

As soon as I heard the news of my son's death, my mind began to scramble. I had a funeral to plan. (This should never happen to a parent.) However, I was very aware of my inexperience at making committal arrangements. And yet the hospital needed to know where to send my son's body. *What were they saying? I wasn't ready to bury my child.*

But in the aftermath I was grateful for sensitive funeral directors who were accommodating and supportive while walking us through the process of preparation and burial.

Subsequent to the death of my son I acquired all available information regarding his accident. I needed to know the truth for myself. Medical reports from ambulance technicians, emergency room doctors and nurses, and other relevant information regarding his short stay in the hospital were then requested. Written reports from police officers at the scene, as well as verbal information, were also obtained.

Although strenuous, oral communication was also part of the process. But the most difficult to grasp was a medical report in graphic form illustrating Matthew's heartbeats until the very last one. A straight line on the heart monitor printout was the hardest to ingest. This report demonstrated his first recorded heartbeats as strong, but within minutes the throbs began to decrease until the final beat.

"Thy dead men shall live, together with my dead body shall they arise. Awake and sing, ye that dwell in dust: for thy dew is as the dew of herbs, and the earth shall cast out the dead" (*Isaiah 26:19*)

The cardiologist's report inspired this poem which indicates a heartbeat's rhythm until the final one, and then it stops forever.

Gone

Gone
Before the cloud could mist
Gone
Before the flick of a wrist

Gone
Before the minute hand moved
Gone
Before your worth had been proved

Gone
After your last breath was drawn
Gone
Before the birds all have flown

Gone
Leaving others standing 'round
Gone
Before hearing the next sound

Gone
After your last heart beat
Gone
No more words left to speak

Gone
No more time to give

Gone
No more life to live

Gone
In the blink of an eye
Gone
Nothing left but to die

© *J. Hannah Lloyd*

Grieving may be a new experience for you. However, while sorting through the maze of emotion, try not to torture yourself as you consolidate your feelings. Realize that your actions will have a strong impact on those around you.

But if you feel out of control, find someone to talk to. It may also help to write your thoughts and feelings in a journal. Putting words on paper could be the best way to express your grief. It's also important to verbalize and not internalize your sorrow.

Don't Want to Know

No...no...no...no
It isn't so
Please don't tell me
Don't want to know

He is not dead
He's just not dead
He just went to
His room instead

"Going to work.
I'm in the zone,"

J. Hannah Lloyd

I hear him call.
"I'm on the phone.

I'll be ready;
Minute or two.
Give me a sec
I'm almost through."

Please don't tell me
Don't want to know
My heart beats fast
My movements slow

Then all comes back
In an awful rush
He is not here
I feel a crush

He truly died
Left me alone
And he is not
Just on the phone

He's not inside
He is no where
My mind tells me
It's just not fair

Yet all my heart
Will not believe
That he's not here
He didn't leave

He's really just
In the next room
My memories say
I'll see him soon

© *J. Hannah Lloyd*

Chapter Twelve

Holidays

Birthdays, anniversaries, and other holidays are all difficult to celebrate following the death of a loved one. The toughest times of sorrow will be the ability to endure these days of celebration.

There are times when you will feel alone in your grief amid the fun and festivity of those around you. But you're not. Millions around the world are also suffering the loss of a loved one. Grief is universal, and unites the inconsolable in one agony of anguish and sorrow.

But hiding your emotions could become a secret addiction if not nipped in the bud. In fact, it's best not to quench your feelings. Allow expressions of grief to occur. Include others who are also grieving, and give yourself time to process your sorrow. This is also beneficial to emotional healing.

The ability to remember joyful moments shared when your loved one was alive will also help to ease the burden of loss. Don't be afraid to grieve. Those moments will be therapeutic, and should improve over time. But as expressed throughout the years, time is the only thing that can ease the load of grief. However, and in most cases, all sorrow doesn't completely go away. It simply becomes easier to accept.

After my son's death I didn't want to celebrate anything. The joy of commemorating the holidays was over. Tears would quickly emerge at any unexpected moment, and sorrow overwhelm when these special days stared me in the face.

It was difficult to lay aside my sorrow just to preserve the traditions of noteworthy holidays. Christmas trees and colorful decorations now lacked appeal, and no longer invited a joyful reunion. And, over time, my stash of Christmas treasure became useless clutter, and then donated to a local thrift store. Only a few possessions remained as a memorial of past traditions and happier times.

Holidays were now only days to hurry through, try to endure, and then disengage from. And because the pain of loss was everywhere, any celebration was difficult to embrace. It was easier to curl up in a blanket and let the world go by.

Yet one tradition remains. At the beginning of each New Year, my calendar is labeled with reminders of birthdays and special days. Even the custom of marking the date of Matt's birth continues. Memories of when he was alive also remain as part of everyday living.

He is, and always will be, an important member of our family.

Holiday Sadness

In the middle of chaos
In the middle of fun
In the middle there is heartache
'Because I'm missing someone

While everyone is busy
And all are having fun
While surrounded by my loved ones
I'm missing that someone

It's always been great joy
When company has come
With lots and lots to do
Still I'm missing that someone

Almost everyone is here
The little ones make it fun
With lots of food and laughter
I'm glad they all could come

But I'm so sad
For the one
Who couldn't come?

© *J. Hannah Lloyd*

Samantha, our granddaughter and Matthew niece, often takes pleasure in watching videos of Uncle Matt, her mother, and her Uncle Austin when they were small. Simply said, she loves the connection. And, as she continues to grow, it's obvious she and Matt share several mutual interests. She also enjoys the notion of their similarities, and mentions her distress at not having her uncle around.

To me her consideration is soothing as she has great appreciation for someone she never had a chance to know. She is also the catalyst for continuation of family traditions as she includes everyone important to her; including all deceased members of her family.

Christmas Gift

By Cathy Pendola

Holidays, especially Christmas, are difficult. The first Christmas after losing Dominic, we put up a tree for my daughter's sake. But we were all choking back the tears. We lit a candle in front of Dom's picture as we opened our gifts. It all felt surreal. I wanted my old life back.

Christmas has always been my favorite holiday and I felt like it was taken away from me. I think holidays, birthdays, and so on require me to do anything that gives me comfort. My son loved Starbucks. Each Christmas I put out his stocking and put a gift card from Starbucks in it. Then I use the card when I go there to remember Dominic, and how we would sometimes meet for coffee before school. I believe everyone, in their own way, finds a coping mechanism to deal with all the reminders of a loss. Slowly you find your way.

Christmas Blur

By Belle Woods

Danny died the Wednesday after Thanksgiving in 2007. Christmas that year remains a blur. I just don't remember much about it, except some friends invited us over to their house, which was a comfort. Being in church and having fellowship with other believers has been one of the biggest supports and encouragements for me, especially during the holidays.

When Danny and I were first married, he was not a fan of Christmas. But I enjoyed Christmas very much. It took a couple of Christmases for Danny to realize it wasn't the way it had been for him as a child. He'd had many bad experiences and didn't want to see Christmas come that first year. But over time he learned to love the holidays as much as I did. I miss him saying, "Merry Christmas, and remember, Jesus is the reason for the season!"

***

Don't be afraid to communicate your feelings to those around you. Your own words of sorrow could encourage others who are also grieving a loss. New friendships have developed when sharing personal stories with people in comparable situations. Individuals grouped in related circumstances can be therapeutic.

It's important not to neglect yourself during this time of grief and restoration. Memories of happier times with your loved one can also help to soften the blow of heartache.

Chapter Thirteen

Remember the Good Times

Matthew could have been a stand-up comic because of his unique ability of bringing laughter to the table. Even as an adult his childlike delight for everything in his world energized those around him. And since laughter is the best medicine, he aimed to please. His invariable creativity was captivating and entertaining.

But when an eight-year-old, he designed a unique Christmas gift for Kyle, his step-dad. His gift was then presented in an oversized cardboard box covered in a colorful array of Scotch, masking, and duct tape. Inside was a designer monstrosity created from a combination of wood, nuts, bolts, cans, and many unnamed scraps of anything he was able to attach.

It didn't have a name or a rational function, but was simply a large and useless conglomerate of cluttered junk. Needless to say, this construction brought unexpected bouts of suppressed laughter that exploded in the room. However, the hours he spent designing this special gift were hard to ignore, and continue to bring unforgettable memories to mind.

***

When a child passes, it becomes even more important to preserve their memory. Pictures and special stories are often the best choice of preservation. Even everyday events are worth the effort to recall. But taking time to write them down could be healing and therapeutic.

After that, they will be available for future enjoyment.

Laughter

He should have been called Isaac
For he was full of fun
From birth to twenty-two
He was the laughing one

His twinkling eyes were bright
Concerns of life ignored
He tried to make you laugh
Your bliss was his reward

Never once forgot a joke
Memory brought them back in rhyme
His satire was the best
Of artists in his time

© *J. Hannah Lloyd*

"A happy heart makes the face cheerful, but heartache crushes the spirit" (*Proverbs 15:13*)
"Even in laughter the heart may ache, and joy may end in grief" (*Proverbs 14: 13*)
"Grieve, mourn and wail. Change your laughter to mourning and your joy to gloom" (*James 4: 9*)

Birthdays, Easter, Thanksgiving, and Christmas can be the most difficult of times following the death of a loved one. The dining room table now has an empty chair. Spontaneous chatter is no longer active. And the heaviness of sorrow is felt by all.

Samantha is missing the love and attention of an uncle she doesn't remember. Austin no longer enjoys the bantering and camaraderie he shared with his brother. And, he doesn't have a younger sibling to recall childhood memories with.

Haley doesn't have the brother she considered more like her in personality than any other family member. And, as parents, we no longer have our youngest to embrace, and lend a hand to.

But Matthew won't be a forgotten uncle, an absent sibling, or a missing family member. We will continue to talk about him as if he were present. Yet the desire to engage in conversation with him, or discuss current events, is a trial that must be dealt with; and even more when holidays are observed.

In the aftermath, memories of the past continue to merge with the present. This exchange, although odd, allows an ongoing connection between brother, uncle, mother, father, and child. And, in this way, our missing loved one remains part of the family circle.

But in reality, a link will always be missing from family gatherings.

Oh, the Memories

Another memory surfaces when Christmas traditions involve the rituals of a visiting Santa Claus.

Christmas was a special time at our house. And, for Matthew, the expectation of Santa's visit was enormous. Each December he would spend hours of time creating a trap to catch the elusive visitor. A maze of kite string tied to door handles, closet knobs, bed posts, and every other piece of large furniture in his bedroom was the plan.

This labyrinth of string would then crisscross the room—wall to wall. Fragments of paper, small toys, and various sundry items were also displayed as decoys throughout the snare. Even cookies and milk had their place, and available for his favorite visitor to enjoy. His plan was to ambush the caller, although his logic for doing so was never quite understood, or revealed. But every year thereafter Santa would maneuvered through the trap to steal the edible treats. And, he always left a note for the designer.

Later, when Matthew learned the truth of Santa's tricks, he remained impervious to that reality. Designing and constructing a new entrapping device then became his own personal Christmas tradition, and continued for several delightful years.

Two Years

Two sad years
Have come and gone
But you're not here
It's been too long

My heart—it aches
For you each day
Ever since
You went away

© *J. Hannah Lloyd*

A Time for Everything
(Ecclesiastes 3:1-8)

"There is a time for everything, and a season for every activity under heaven:
A time to be born and a time to die, a time to plant and a time to uproot,
A time to kill and a time to **heal**, a time to tear down and a time to build,
A time to **weep** and a time to laugh, a time to **mourn** and
A time to dance,
A time to scatter stones and a time to gather them,
A time to embrace and a time to refrain, a time to search and a time to give up,
A time to keep and a time to throw away, a time to tear and a time to mend,
A time to be silent and a time to speak, a time to love and a time to hate,
A time for war and a time for peace"

Birthday

Today was my son's birthday
But he won't celebrate
It's time for one more birthday
But now it is too late

More birthdays will come and go
But never quite the same
The age of twenty-two
He always will remain

© *J. Hannah Lloyd*

Chapter Fourteen

When a Child Dies

"**A** voice is heard in Ramah, weeping and great mourning, Rachel weeping for her children and refusing to be comforted, because they are no more" *(Matthew 2:18)*

Losing a child in death can easily be the most devastating experience of a lifetime. If your child was stillborn, or lived to be ninety years of age, he is still your flesh and blood. A part of you will then die when your child does.

Death is cruel, and the after effects painful. Yet age has no bearing on this certainty. The emotional aspects of your loss can be catastrophic.

When a child you've waited for, cuddled, dressed, fed, and loved with every ounce of your being dies, it's enough to make any parent go insane. Although my child was twenty-two when he passed, he was still my baby. That truth will always be our bond.

"Remember not the sins of my youth and my rebellious ways; according to your love remember me, for you are good, oh Lord" *(Psalms 25:7)*

***

J. Hannah Lloyd

A Part of Me

Close to my heart
But still in my womb
I was there with you
Until you were born

Then I was there
To hold you long,
And kiss you gently
With lullaby song

I was there for you
As you nursed my breast
Then lay your head
Upon my chest

And slept that soft
Gentle baby sleep
As you dreamed I prayed
Your soul to keep

I was there for you
When you stumped your toe
I watched you learn
And watched you grow

So thankful was I
But you couldn't yet see
I'll love you always
You are a part of me

Then without warning you were killed
But how could I have known
Your life would end this way
And you would die alone?

© *J. Hannah Lloyd*

Although it's best to move on with your life following the death of a child, this blind in-your-face reality makes that notion impossible. In fact, the term *time heals all wounds* will never fit parental bereavement. This exception relates to the death of a child far more than any other loss. In fact, the reverse connotation is more accurate as more intense sorrow will surface as time goes on. However, to understand this truth is to accept the verity of death.

But when a child is involved, there is no moving forward. Horror and grief are moments that will surround a parent for days and months, even years following the passing of a child. In the aftermath, and for a prolonged period of time, it will be impossible to budge from this sorrow. Survival is accomplished only while anesthetized and numb every waking moment of every meaningless day.

Anguish over the death of your own flesh-and-blood offspring can lead to mental de-fragmentation of all sanity. This torment will be even more grueling, time-consuming, and painful as time goes forward.

In *Mourning and Melancholia (1917)* Sigmund Freud makes a famous distinction between mourning, which is the normal reaction to the loss of a loved one, and melancholia, which is a form of mental illness. According to Freud grieving people need to break free from the deceased, let go of the past, and begin again by going in a different direction.

A healthy grief experience, according to Freud, is one in which the deaths of loved ones will not leave traces of any gross change in the bereaved. However, his concept has been proven false.

Psychologists are now realizing the importance of maintaining bonds with the deceased, and demonstrate that a lifetime of grief is normal in cases of loss following the death of close friends and family members. This sorrow is even deeper when a child has died.

***

God's Comfort

God's peace that passes all understanding was my only sanity during the days and months that followed the death of my son. He was in control even though I wasn't. His comfort was evident, and covered my grief with quiet serenity. Yet never before had I experienced such calming presence. But as promised in God's word, the Holy Spirit surrounded me, and hovered near; bringing peace and tranquility to my crushed and shattered soul.

"...to comfort all who mourn" *(Isaiah 61:2)*

Satan tried to interject thoughts of Hell into my mind to torture me. But when I said, "Satan get behind me. Do *not* taunt me," his harassment stopped.

"And the peace of God, which transcends all understanding, will guard your hearts and your minds in Christ Jesus" (Philippians 4:7)
"Peace I leave with you; my **peace** I give you..." (John 14:27)
"...who comforts us in all our troubles, so that we can **comfort** those in any trouble with the **comfort** we ourselves have received from God" *(2 Corinthians 1:4)*

Where is Assurance?

Do you need reassurance? The Bible provides verses of comfort to those who morn.
"You will keep in perfect peace him whose mind is steadfast, because he trusts in you" *(Isaiah 26:3)*
"...as a mother comforts her child, so will I comfort you; and you will be comforted..." *(Isaiah 66:13)*
...I will turn their mourning into gladness; I will give them comfort and joy instead of sorrow" *(Jeremiah 31:13)*

God is With Me

I know that God is with me
I know he truly cares
I know he'll never leave me
I know he's always there

I know for his Spirit
Reminds me where I'm from
Assures me that I'm safe
And that I'll overcome

He brings me peace of mind
When my world falls apart
Then places joy within me,
And puts love in my heart

When deepest sorrow comes
That takes my sleep at night
I feel his Spirit with me
And he whispers, "It's all right."

© *J. Hannah Lloyd*

"Be merciful to me, O Lord, for I am in distress; my eyes grow weak with sorrow, my soul and my body with grief" *(Psalms 31:9)*

Never have I understood why Matthew had to die so young. Before his death, many prayers were prayed for his protection. And because my prayers were faith based, I lived with the confidence that angels would hover near and respond when needed.

My belief was strong because many times God had answered my prayers. Faith had also seen me through an abusive childhood, and violent first marriage. Surely he would see me through this tragedy.

Answered Prayer

Our family once planned a trip from West Tennessee, where we lived, to North Carolina to visit family and friends when Matt was seventeen and Austin nineteen. But since both boys wanted to drive their own cars, Kyle and I conceded—with reservation. Neither had driven nonstop for seven hours straight.

We all began the trip as a convoy of three. But near Nashville traffic tightened, and our cars were separated as more vehicles flooded the highway. Panic again seized my mind as fear overtook my senses.

Austin was driving in front, still in sight, but Matt had long before disappeared; and I began to pray, and pray, and pray.

Minutes later Kyle exited the highway for a brief refueling. And there, standing at the gas pump, was Matthew; grinning from ear to ear. Heart in throat, I poured out my thanksgiving to God for this incredible miracle. Yet that was only one of many answered prayers. But after his death I had to ask myself, was it reasonable to be angry with God for his demise?

The answer is still, "No."

July 28

To Matthew from Mom

Ten years ago
This very day
You left this world
And went away

I see you run
Without a care
Arms open wide
A hug to share

Your smile so clear
With shy allure
I miss you so
There is no cure

© *J. Hannah Lloyd*

Because God honored my desire for children, Matthew was born. And although his life ended after twenty-two years, God had kept him safe many times during his life. But now, without God's mercy, I had no desire to live—not another day, or another minute. And yet I continued to trust in Him. There was no one else.

Still, it was natural for me to believe in God. I always had. However, I was amazed that my sanity remained intact following the death of my son. But I was concerned for the rest of the family; my other children and my husband. How would they react to this tragedy? What were they feeling? And how could I help them?

Haley and her husband were scheduled to finalize the purchase of their new home the morning Matthew was killed. But after the news their plan changed. It was then decided our granddaughter Samantha would stay with us at our house while they completed their acquisition. Also, the following day was her third birthday. However, and because we were all in shock, decisions made at that time seemed logical considering the circumstances.

Haley and Samantha then drove to our home in Charlotte, arriving around nine o'clock that morning. Our original plan was to drive to the funeral home as soon as they arrived. But since our church pastor earlier promised to be with us, we decided to wait until his arrival; and then go. However, a few minutes past eleven the church secretary called, and informed us the pastor would not be coming.

Then realizing precious minutes had been squandered, we jumped in the car and drove to the designated funeral home, about three hours away. We needed to see Matthew one last time, and make arrangements for his funeral.

Etched forever in infinity, this day was the most horrible one ever lived. Every excruciating moment was surreal. Not only was my child dead, but my trust in a cleric compromised.

Later, following our visit to the morgue, we drove to the home of Ashley, my ex-husband's sister, and the aunt of my children. Their home would be the designated receiving station for family and friends.

An amazing abundance of prepared food from Matthew's employment, local churches, neighbors and friends of the family had been provided. Several flower arrangements had already been delivered. The dining room table also revealed a huge spread of delicious cuisine for all to enjoy. I don't recall eating one bite.

The following day Haley drove to town to meet her husband at the attorney's office to complete the purchase of their new home. What she remembers most, following the news of her brother's death, was driving many hours as she traveled between several states in order to complete her commitments.

Austin had been scheduled to take important test in college the day his brother was killed, but decided to remain as testing was difficult to re-schedule. Then later that morning he and two of his friends drove from Tennessee to our home. But their communication was minimal during the trip. Austin simply preferred not to speak, or to think. He only wanted to get home and be with his family.

Details of that day remain blurred. But Kyle, my husband, was a solid rock as, together, we plunged headlong into our nightmare.

The Way it is

"I felt horrible for the way Matthew died," Kyle said. "I felt deep sorrow that he was so young. But he was gone and I could do nothing for him. I also felt sorry for you, his mother. I saw how painful this was for you. Matthew was your child, and the youngest. He was your baby.

Timing was also a factor. When Matt died your relationship with him was strained. My heart went out to you. I ached for you.

But now, after years of grieving, everyone else has

moved on; but not you. No one will ever grieve over your son like you will. You are his mom. And because a mother's love runs deep, you will never stop grieving for him. And, that's just the way it is."

But for God's Mercy

"...he will never leave you nor forsake you" *(Deuteronomy 31:8)*

Why should I praise God now? My youngest was dead. Where was God's mercy when he died?

I admit there were times when I felt the answer to my prayers was a bit slow in coming. But God had always been faithful. Every day, after Matthew's death, I would breathe a quick word of praise. "Thank you for your mercy," had long been my daily words of gratitude.

Over the years God had answered many prayers for me. He'd made it clear he was my help, and strength. The test of time had also proven him faithful. But what about this time? What about now?

Its true God never promised to take away my problems. He only promised to be with me *through* them. Trust is what I had to do.

Again, following the crushing blow of my son's death I tested God once more. "Thank you for your mercy," I said in a faint whisper.

Then, in an instant, there was God—bringing waves of comfort to surround me like a warm, fuzzy blanket. It was then I discovered that whatever happens in life, God would be with me. His love and mercy would surround me because I trusted in Him. And that's a promise I can live with.

"Thank you God for your mercy that is new every morning. Amen."

Bad News

When we received the news of my son's death, our family had yet to realize the magnitude of what was ahead. The news was implausible, mind-boggling, and difficult to grasp.

Still in a daze, we all operated in mechanical despondency while trying to comprehend the unbelievable. Those moments are still difficult to recall although more than ten years have passed since that terrible day.

Away

Gone, yet not forgotten
Although you are away
Your love forever keeps me
Each and every day

© J. Hannah Lloyd

Chapter Fifteen

Sharing the Pain

There's nothing more gripping than personal stories of sorrow and survival. And, there's nothing more real than visualizing sorrow when combined with understanding and sympathy. However, by sharing complicated times, new friendships often develop with others who are also grieving similar losses.

Several contributors provided stories for this book that are worth sharing. They are integrated throughout this book. Below are more.

Losing my Son Dominic

By Cathy Pendola

I lost my wonderful son Dominic in a car accident in 2004. He was nineteen years old and had his whole life in front of him; or so I thought. I still can't believe he's gone. Losing a child changes the landscape of your life forever.

The first year after losing Dominic I felt like I was walking around in a fog. I would get up each day and reality would hit me in the face the moment I opened my eyes. I did what I needed to do to get through the day. But some days I could barely take a shower. I wanted to stay in the house, be alone, and shut out the world. Week-ends were especially hard because that was our time to be together as a family. But now a member of our family was missing. It was just my husband, daughter, and me sitting at a dinner table for four. We had to watch the waiter clear away the fourth place setting because no one would be joining us. Life goes on but I felt as if I was standing still, watching.

Sometimes I wonder how my family and I have survived this tragedy. What I have learned is this is a day-to-day, one-foot-in-front-of-the-other process.

Reading has helped me. The books I can't get enough of are about near death experiences, and life after death. I know these are not books most people would want to read. But somehow they give me comfort. On some level I'm searching for what this whole *after-life* thing is all about. I also know I'm looking for answers to a question that cannot be given in this life...why? Sometimes things happen that we have no control over, and no explanation for.

It has been ten years now since I lost my son. And yes, time gives me perspective. I don't believe time heals all wounds—at least not this wound. What I've learned is to cherish everyone around you that you love. Tell them you love them, and often. Appreciate all the moments you have together, and live in the moment. Life is wonderful, but fragile. We should handle it with care.

Double Sorrow

By Alison McCall

My cell phone rang at 6:00 a.m. just as I was getting ready to shower for work on Monday October 8, 2012. It's never a good feeling when a call comes that early. But when I saw it was from my son Ben, a musician night owl who never gets up early, I immediately felt sick; and knew something was terribly wrong. His voice was shaky and he was crying.

But his words literally brought me to the floor. "Mom, Jeremy is dead."

Absolute shock and intense horror immediately hit me like a ton of bricks. I knew my younger son had not been doing well as of late. In the past he'd struggled with heroin as an addiction, and recently been cited for DUI. But dead! No, this just could NOT be true! Arrested and in jail—yes, that I could possibly accept. But deceased? No way! The shock, the grief, and the anguish were totally overwhelming.

My husband Buddy was lying in bed when I got the call. He was undergoing chemotherapy for cancer at the time. But my sobs brought him out of bed as I began to try, in some way, to tell him what was going on. I could not stand. I could not think. This could not be true. Oh God help me! My precious baby could not be dead!

Buddy called my boss to let him know what had happened, and that I would not be at work. Then, in robot mode, I dressed for the drive to Charlotte where Jeremy's dad and step-mom lived. Jeremy had recently lived with them to get his life together. But in the past few days he'd moved back with his old roommate; apparently to resume his heroin usage.

As Buddy drove us to Charlotte, I placed the call to my sisters and friends—all the while thinking this could not possibly be true. The sobs then came as reality set in.

In Charlotte our blended family came together to cry, plan, and talk. A special song *If I Were a Butterfly* was chosen for Jeremy's memorial from his preschool days to be played as the family was seated. But when his step-mom and I were on the front porch saying good-by, a beautiful butterfly flew right up to her face, and then flew over my parked car and hovered. *Was that Jeremy?* All we knew was that it was sweet sign for us as we hugged.

But my thoughts while driving home were intense with sadness and fear. How in God's name could I deal with the death of my son as well as care for my dying husband? I even questioned God's goodness and love. Where was God in all of this? I felt lost, guilty, even self-hatred. What could I have done to help save Jeremy? Surely this was my fault. At Jeremy's memorial service Buddy had to sit during the family visitation due to his weakness from chemotherapy. He was white as snow and had no hair. I felt as if my mind and spirit were breaking, and that I couldn't possibly take all that was happening. Periods of intense, uncontrollable, and guttural sobs would come, but there was no comfort or relief—just pain and disbelief.

Later, on April 2, 2013—only six months since Jeremy's untimely death—my husband Buddy took his last breath in our bed, with me by his side. Again, denial and shock overtook my mind. However, by this time, I couldn't handle my reality. My old nemesis anorexia now had full control of my life.

But if I couldn't control the deaths of my son and my husband, than surely I could control my weight—an issue that had long been with me but sky-rocketed with the loss of son and my husband. My weight also plummeted to 76 pounds, and my disease of alcoholism again reared its ugly head again.

I had no coping skills to deal with the intense pain in my heart. Although I had an awesome support group, and family love beyond belief; I was unable to reach out. Intense treatment was then required to help get my health and life back together. Finally I was able to reach out to God for help, and to those around me that He so richly blessed me with.

Time has gone by, and the grief—well, all I can say is that it is different. Yet I do not blame God for either Jeremy or Buddy's death, and neither do I blame myself. But reaching out to other moms who've lost a child, and other wives who've also lost a husband brings the greatest relief. One day at a time life, for me, goes on. I do know that my life will never be the same, but often ask God for help; and know that He wants to use me, in some way, to help others.

Jeremy was 24 years old when he died. He was an awesome chess player and chef. He was excelling at his job and had just received a promotion. And when he was young he played baseball quite well and as a teen he played soccer very well.

Buddy never lost his deep faith in God and his wonderful sense of humor. He even had the hospice nurses laughing at his stories. He also ordered Bible Promises books by the case, and continued sharing these with others until the end of his life.

He seldom complained, even when he was house bound; although he was the type of person who hated staying home as he loved getting out and meeting friends for lunch.

My husband and my son are greatly missed.

Our Little Missionary

By Carolyn K. Knefely

Little Miss Missionary
With death comes life
With loss comes gain
With Christ comes comfort
In bearing the pain

©. *Carolyn K. Knefely*

Breathing was a struggle for our newborn daughter, Carrie. Without a pallet or esophagus, taking nourishment between her tiny lips was impossible. So many other things went wrong because her body had given her one gene too many.

Leaning down the doctor cleared his throat. "No heroics will change the outcome," he said. Carrie was given less than eight hours to live. He pronounced death, but Christ delivered life. Our little missionary lived eleven days.

Through Carrie's death I found new life in walking closer to Jesus Christ. I hadn't read the Bible until dealing with her death, and the lonely days that followed. Reaching daily for comfort in the word of God, I gained new reasons to live. Now I celebrate Carrie's life even though it was short. I praise God for taking her because His little girl is now whole in His arms.

Losing my Nephew

By Leigh Ann Carter

My oldest sister Sandra lost her first born son in a car wreck on Mother's Day when he was twenty-one. Another sister Mary's first born son was in the same wreck. I always call it the wreck instead of an automobile accident because of the wreckage it leaves in the hearts and lives of those left behind.

Sandra was called to the hospital and told her son had died. Upon arrival she learned her son was not the one who had died because she recognized his voice as he screamed in the emergency room. Her son lived but Mary's son died at the scene. This accident was about twenty-five years ago. Mary is still a bitter, angry woman. Sandra has always found relief in a bottle. So does her son, the one who survived the accident. In a way, we all died that day.

Of ten children, eight of us had sons as our first born. One had a son as her second born, and one didn't have children at all.

There are many hurting people who don't know how to deal with grief. They need someone who knows the depth of their suffering and can to minister to them. Those of us who are fortunate enough to have raised our first born are called the lucky ones. We are locked out of the hearts of those who have suffered the ultimate loss. We're unable to reach the place that aches. In a way, we can't understand. But God never allows us to suffer without a reason.

***

With the passing of a loved one, bitterness and depression may become your reality. However, if feelings of despair settle in and remain, consulting a minister or professional may be essential. But remember. There's no shame in requesting this type of help as depression is a natural process of grieving.

The possibility of re-occurring depression could be predictable. But, over time, your depressive feelings should pass, and a more positive outlook become your position.

***

More than ten years have now passed since Matthew was killed. And yet there are times when sorrow is still brutally harsh. It still rips through my heart, and shreds it to pieces. And it still feels his death has just happened. But there is also peace in knowing that God is in control over everything that has happened, and will happen. And the peace that passes all understanding is all that keeps me grounded, and from losing my mind when my focus becomes distorted, and sadness again claims each waking moment.

—J. Hannah Lloyd

Chapter Sixteen

When a Spouse Dies

Losing a spouse in death is the same as losing a part of you. What was joined together has now been divided. This sorrow is also a severe invasion in your life. Memories will now surround you from every direction, with no resolution in sight.

The common is now uncommon. And what was normal no longer is. Your bed is empty, and your soul-mate missing. You will also realize the dining room table was built for more than one. Your helper is gone, and your entire pattern of life has changed. You're now alone.

Problems of forgetfulness may set in. In the past you may have been organized, but after the death of your spouse that focus has changed.

Disorganization and forgetfulness are normal following the death of a loved one. But when appointments are missed, keys misplaced, and routine activities forgotten, poor memory and aggravation may become bothersome. Your struggle to conquer the sadness of losing your beloved will now consume the mind.

Try to be patient with yourself. Write notes as reminders of future scheduled appointments for reference when absentmindedness sets in. And don't be afraid to ask for help if you feel overwhelmed.

Routine tasks may now take longer to complete than normal. Even the ability to manage time effectively may surface as projects remain unfinished.

Learn to design your time wisely so important things are planned, thus making tasks easier to complete.

Then focus on new outlets that will help to ease your sense of loneliness. Don't become isolated from others as interaction with friends and family is crucial for recovering from the emotions of sorrow. It's important to function well in order to continue living your life to the fullest.

A Widow Mourns

My mother was somewhat independent until my father passed away. A short time later she became edgy and fearful. Her phobia then escalated until it was necessary to install an alarm system, complete with sensors and motion detectors. Even after installation she retained long term distrust in people.

Routine household noises were all cause for anxiety. And although she talked about her fears with everyone, she was unable to forget them. She lived in a safe environment, but that alone couldn't bring her peace of mind.

My father had always serviced her car with oil changes and tire checks. His diligence also maintained their property by mowing the lawn, raking leaves, and removing broken branches when necessary. He also kept the interior and exterior of the home repaired.

The household was functional as long as he was live. But following his death, several close neighbors needed to step in, and assist with the outdoor tasks she wasn't able to herself complete.

Although my mother was blessed with an abundance of friends and family, she was never able to release her fears. She strongly missed the man she'd always depended on, but taken for granted. But after his death, she learned how difficult it was to be a widow.

Although she refused to talk about her loneliness, her actions demonstrated her need for companionship, assistance, and support.

***

While issues of burial, finances, and loneliness are being resolved, painful memories may be difficult to surrender. But, over time, most sad moments should fade as warm and happier memories again surface.

The heart will always hold a place for your beloved. Yet when it takes more time than expected to sort through those feelings, therapy or counseling with a cleric or professional counselor may be beneficial. But realize it's often easier to accept help from a professional than a family member or close friend.

Many questions will surface after your loved one is laid to rest. Who will be my helpmate now? Can I survive by myself? Who will assist me in the yard, or with the house? Who will prepare my meals? Who will take care of my finances? And who can I depend on now? These questions and more will invade the mind and may cause anxiety.

But now is the time to accept help from others. Don't shun their help, and don't be afraid to ask for it either. Let their assistance be your comfort. Then allow God to be a husband or wife for you. Only he can fill that void with his comfort, and give you peace.

Who Will?

When I'm feeling sad,
Who will bring me cheer?
And when I'm all alone
Who is always near?

When I am crying
Who will wipe my tears?
And when I am scared
Who will calm my fears?

When I am hurting
Who will feel my pain?
And when I am senseless
Who makes me feel sane?

When I am hungry
Who will give me food?
And when I'm in despair
Who will calm my mood?

When I am in danger,
Who will keep me safe?
And when I need a shelter
Who gives me a place?

When I am confused,
Who will understand?
And when I am dying
Who will hold my hand?

Jesus knows and feels
Everything I feel
Jesus calms my fears
For he is very real

© *J. Hannah Lloyd*

"The **widow** who is really in need and left all alone puts her hope in God and continues night and day to pray and to ask God for help" *(I Timothy 5:5)*

"Then you will call, and the Lord will answer; you will cry for help, and he will say: "Here am I" *(Isaiah 58:9)*

"Hear my prayer, O Lord, listen to my cry for help; be not deaf to my weeping" *(Psalms 39:12)*

"In my distress I called to the Lord; I cried to my God for help" *(Psalms 18: 6)*

"But you, O Lord, be not far off; O my Strength, come quickly to help me" *(Psalms 22: 19)*

"Yet I am poor and needy; may the Lord think of me. You are my help and my deliverer; O my God, do not delay" *(Psalms 40:17)*

"Surely God is my help; the Lord is the one who sustains me" *(Psalms 54:4)*

"Let us then approach the throne of grace with confidence, so that we may receive mercy and find grace to help us in our time of need" *(Hebrews 4:16)*

Dust

You were real
I could feel
Flesh and blood
I could touch
Now just dust

Lost in pain
Little gain
Only rain
Can't refrain
Who to blame

No more trust
Death a bust
Ashes to ashes
Dirt and rust
Now you're gone

You're just dust

© *J. Hannah Lloyd*

"By the sweat of your brow you will eat your food until you return to the ground, since from it you were taken; for **dust** you are and to **dust** you will return" *(Genesis 3:19)*

Losing my Husband

By Belle Woods

When Danny died I lost my best friend. We were friends before we became engaged, and were inseparable. It has been over three years now, but it's still fresh. His death left a hole in my heart and in my life. During the night I wake up thinking he's still asleep beside me, but I just find an empty pillow. Then the loneliness sets in. The only thing that helps is talking to the Lord. So I do until I fall back asleep.

I've had two gardening seasons since Danny passed away, but I'm not so sure about this year. The first year was very difficult. Danny wasn't an outdoor person, but he'd always helped me with the garden. In the evening, just before sunset we'd go *walk together in the garden in the cool of the evening* to see how it was progressing. Last summer it was difficult for me to spend time in the garden. It was such a lonely place without him.

Going to Wal-Mart was difficult because the last eight years of Danny's life we were together twenty-four-seven, which meant we always went shopping together. Even after almost thirty years of marriage, I'd look up and see him come around the corner from an isle and my heart would skip a few beats. I just loved him so much. Going shopping wasn't fun anymore. Three months after he died a new Wal-Mart opened up. It's easier to shop there because the surroundings have changed.

My sleep had been insufficient several years before he died because I have Fibromyalgia. But after he died it became worse. I would go for nights without sleep, or I would cry myself to sleep. I asked my Aunt Eva, who had lost her husband, "How long was it before you stopped crying yourself to sleep?"

She couldn't tell me. But I cried every night for over a year. Now it happens less frequently.

One of the hardest things to do is to help people understand why I have no desire to seek out another relationship. I have well-meaning friends who've known me for over thirty years, but think I should call an old friend (who had planned to ask me to marry him but Danny asked me first). This man then married a very nice girl and they had two children, and adopted two. She died from cancer about three years before Danny. And now this man is widowed. These well-meaning friends think I should call him. But I can't. How can I think of starting another relationship when I'm still in love?

Some people have asked me if I am mad at God. My reply is, "If God is my problem there is no answer." I never was angry or upset with God. I did get angry with the doctor but the Lord told me right away, being angry at her was not beneficial for me. So I chose to forgive her.

The Lord has been there for me through it all, and He has supplied my every need. He even worked miracles for me at my bank, the insurance company, and for my personal wellbeing. Peace has been a daily blessing from the Lord. I can't praise Him enough for being there with me every step of the way. And I know He will be with me forever.

Chapter Seventeen

When a Parent Dies

Facing the death of a parent often leaves a child, grown or otherwise, with a sense of the inevitable. But now is the time to understand you reign as a member of the next generation. It will also be a time of reflection as you realize your dependency on your parent is now over.

Never again will there be discussions of the future, or chats about the past. No longer will assistance be given as all communication has now ceased. Your parent's life is complete, and over. Although their death may have been expected, this reality will still be crushing. It most certainly will be a time of reflection.

The Next Generation

We looked all around
At older ones together
Laughing with each other
Sharing memories of forever

Now a few is all there is
To keep the family station
But when they're dead and gone
We're the next generation

© *J. Hannah Lloyd*

Sometimes sorrow is delayed for the remaining parent as they try to protect and console their children. But when the truth hits, tremendous stress and anxiety will surely surface for all involved.

However, as a resource, plan to offer the remaining parent assistance when needed. Then be prepared to take charge. Also remember to take care of yourself during the hours and days following the loss of your parent. This bereavement will affect not only you, but your siblings and the remaining parent in unexpected ways.

Allow God to be your strength and comfort as others reach out to you in sympathy and understanding.

Scars

The scars of life
Within—without
But deep within
Leaves not a doubt

To be the scar
That makes me mad
That causes grief
And makes life sad

A scratch, a bump
A cut, a scrape
Takes time to heal
Not time to make

The scars of life
Have left me broken
Have never mended
Yet are not spoken

© *J. Hannah Lloyd*

If you are the adult child of a bereaved parent, your concern for that parent is essential. But realize, not only have you lost a parent but your remaining parent has lost a spouse, and may need more understanding than is normal.

Often a grieving mind will wander while struggling to overcome the loss of a partner. The inability to concentrate while driving can also be a dangerous activity for them, and others. They may also be unsuccessful at staying focused while reading, eating, or watching television. But if their actions become bothersome, now is the time for someone to step up and take control of the situation.

A parent's failure to retain what they read or see can also be alarming. But as their caregiver, your patience will go a long way. Offer help with routine tasks such as mowing the lawn or handling dangerous equipment until your parent is again able to function in a normal way.

Unexpected bouts of crying or an inability to handle sorrow may now require more interaction from others. Depression and lack of self-motivation may also set in. But if that is the case, try to provide positive reinforcement for your parent, and contact a doctor if their emotional distress gets out of hand. Also be aware of potential dangers such as over-usage of drugs and alcohol. Offer help and support when needed, and encourage your parent to express themselves verbally. Discussing their grief will also help to ease their sorrow, and yours. Hopefully, and over time, a more positive outlook will emerge.

Continue to trust in God for guidance as you and your remaining parent and sibling(s) overcome the sorrow of losing your loved one.

Later the disposal of a parent's possessions will be disturbing. Your childhood will then come back to haunt you. Memories will also surface that had long been forgotten. However, this can also be a time of resolution. Deciding to be the best you can be for the time you have left will be redeeming.

Try to remember the good times as they may bring feelings of pleasure and sincere appreciation for your recently deceased parent. It can also be a time of re-thinking your own choices and desires. Admiration for your departed parent can help to establish your own determination of continuing to make your parents proud.

But if you had a strained relationship with a deceased parent, now is the time to forgive, and forget.

My Dad

By Lori Marett

My dad was given six to twelve months to live. He divided that time up and lived another nine months. It was cancer. I pretty much said goodbye to him when he started losing his faculties. The man I saw two weeks before he passed was not my dad. The last week he was comatose. So when the funeral came I didn't cry. To this day I have not wept for my father. I had a great relationship with him and knew he was whole again and in heaven. So I've not grieved the loss.

The rest of my family grieved, but I have not. Only a handful of times does a tear slip down my cheek when I think of something special we shared. But other than that, I rejoice at the passing of my father and can't wait to see him again. Now, if I were to lose one of my daughters to cancer; that would be a totally different story. For my dad, there really wasn't any grieving on my part. I know that probably sounds weird...

***

In the Night Season

In the night season
I need a reason
To hold on

It won't be long
'Till He appears
Oh, so near

In the night season
He is my reason
To live

© *J. Hannah Lloyd*

Grieving my Mother

By Ann Tatlock

The call came early in the morning on August 1, 1985. As soon as I heard the phone ring, I knew who it was and what he was going to tell me. It would be my father calling long-distance from the hospital in Illinois, and he would tell me my mother had died.

Mom had been undergoing cancer treatment for eighteen months. Her death was not unexpected and yet, when Dad told me she was gone, I was devastated. Mom and I had always had a close, loving relationship; she was my confidant, the first person to whom I turned to share both the good and bad moments of my life.

The grief I experienced following her death ran deep, with all the usual feelings of loss and sadness. But at the same time I experienced a certain restlessness I didn't expect, and found it hard to identify. I often sensed that something was left undone; there was someone I needed to talk to, something I needed to say....and then I would understand. I simply wanted to talk with Mom, and she wasn't there.

Mom had been a constant presence in my life for twenty-five years, but all that was over now. We'd been separated by the finality of death. I wouldn't be talking with her anymore, not in this life, not until heaven.

But heaven, I realized, was the important thing. I was in one of those life situations where the rubber meets the road, where I couldn't coast by on merely empty words. My faith in God's promises had to be real, because God himself is real and good and unchanging. Did I believe in heaven? Did I believe that Mom, though she had died, was still alive in the very presence of God?

Yes. I did believe. And it was not a vague wish but a true knowing that Mom *still was,* and that though I couldn't see and be with her now, one day I would be with her again.

By this time in my life I was a freelance writer of non-fiction articles, and I was working on my master's degree in journalism. With Mom's death I felt compelled to find a new way to express both my grief and the hope I have in Jesus. I started writing my first novel, a fictional story based on Mom's experiences in the hospital.

That novel was never published, but it was a turning point in my career. I knew God was calling me in a direction I hadn't before considered: to use fiction as a vehicle for revealing truth, for telling about His plan of salvation and eternal life. Now, many years and several novels later, whenever a reader tells me a book of mine renewed her faith or inspired her in some way, I know God used my grief to put me in the position of passing hope on to others.

***

Remembering a parent's witty character in a humorous way can also be another way of coping with their death. My mother would have enjoyed her great granddaughter's fiasco at her funeral had she been alive to witness it. The innocent actions of a child can bring laughter to a grieving family even though the occasion may be very sad.

Losing my Parents

Both of my parents were devout Christians, but raised their children with a firm hand. My father was the first to pass away. He was eighty-years-old when he died of cancer. He was buried at the Veterans Cemetery in honor of his military service. My mother passed away eleven years later, and was buried with him.

They both lived through the depression era but didn't like to talk about it. My father served the military in both Army and Navy during World War II. But as a sailor, he was shipwrecked and dumped into the ocean. Although he survived the cold and murky darkness of the water amid serious threats of shark attacks, he was forever changed. Later, after the war, he remained edgy, nervous, and tense. And, over time, he was unable to work a public job; and became a full-time farmer.

The relationship with my father was minimal. He didn't want children and remained somewhat aloof and distant during my childhood. Although he required hard labor from his family on the farm, his input into my raising, other than teaching me the word of God, was almost non-existent. However, before he died he managed to say he loved me, although it was a struggle.

My mother read Bible stories and other books to me when I was small. But she loved the Bible best. Over time her health deteriorated, and her last two years were spent in a nursing home. She died of a heart attack at the age of eighty-six. Yet her life was long, and evidence that loving

God had been her priority.

Both parents vigorously taught me the word of God. And, they lived it. Because of them I am a Christian today.

"Honor your father and mother—which is the first commandment with a promise—that it may go well with you and that you may enjoy long life on the earth" *(Ephesians 6:2)*

The Epitaph on their gravestones is a reminder of their devout faith.

Resting from my labored past (his)
Home in Jesus' arms at last (hers)

© *J. Hannah Lloyd*

Tribute to Great-Grandmother

Standing in a reception line at her great-grandmother's funeral, seven-year-old Samantha was obviously bored, and quite fidgety. But as relatives and friends filed past, shaking hands or hugging family members, she realized she was also included in this strange and unusual ritual. Then joining in, she firmly extended her small hand in anticipation of the next hand-shaker, and her countenance radiated with exuberance.

"Nana, tell those people over there to come over here and shake our hands," she said in hushed tones as she pointed her finger at a small group huddled nearby, deeply engaged in conversation. She then extended her hand to the lady next in line. "I saw you play the piano," she said. "I play the guitar."

The lady looked surprised as she shook Samantha's hand, as did others standing in line. But it was obvious Samantha had found her niche'.

Later, following a luncheon provided by the church, our family drove a short distance to the chapel at the veteran's cemetery for the graveside portion of the funeral. But while waiting for everyone to take their places inside, Samantha spotted some flags lined up in front. Allowing her curiosity to lead, she sprinted to the front to examine them at closer range.

"Are these state flags?" she asked.

"No, they're Army, Navy, Air Force, and Marine; and that's the Christian flag at the end," I said in a whisper as she pointed to each one. Then realizing she needed something else to distract her, and noticing the American flag nearby, I signaled her attention. "Samantha, why don't you lead everyone in the pledge of allegiance? Then you can sit down because the pastor will be here in a minute to complete Great-Grandmother's funeral."

Unafraid and always ready to entertain, she dashed to the podium and stood as tall as she could behind it. She then lifted her small hands in a standing gesture and, with authority in her voice, asked everyone to stand. Then placing her right hand over her heart, she began to recite in perfect dialogue, "I pledge allegiance to the flag of the United States of America..."

And, without missing a beat, everyone joined in; voices swelling with amazing American patriotism that gently echoed around the rock walls of the veteran's chapel.

What a patriotic way to complete a funeral service," "*What better send-off could one get?*

Later, after the funeral as everyone filed out of the chapel, Samantha asked, "Grandpa, how did they get Great-Grandmother in that little box?"

Then, as a way of explaining cremation to a child, Kyle said, "They shrunk her down, and then put her in the box."

Still curious, she asked, "How did they shrink her?"

"They put her in a big oven that made her shrink," he said, hoping this would be understandable to her.

"How hot was the oven?" she asked, a curious look on her face.

"I don't know," he said.

"Was it three hundred degrees?"

"Probably something like that," he said, and grimaced; hoping this uncomfortable conversation would soon end.

"Oh, just like baking cookies," she said, and giggled. Then satisfied with his answer, she bounded toward the car and more interesting matters.

Chapter Eighteen

When a Child Loses a Parent

Following the death of a family member everyone, including children, will feel incomplete and splintered as their world has now been shattered. But the desire to withdraw from each other in order to address personal grief is normal. However, it's important that a child, or children, not feel disconnected from the rituals of death and burial. Try to stay linked in with them, and address their grief in order to alleviate any fear they may have of the unknown.

Children need to talk about what has happened following the death of a parent. The ability to share their account with others will be both therapeutic and healing. It's also important to listen closely to their words in order to validate their emotions. Over time the child will have more understanding of their parent's death and, as time allows, the ability to move on with their life. Utilizing the same tools is also necessary if a child loses a sibling, or other significant family member.

Try to maintain daily routines with your child whenever possible. Inform schools, teachers, parents of friends, and other activity leaders of the death so they are aware, and able provide added support when needed.

Remember to share hugs and words of encouragement with your child several times a day. Also give them a chance to communicate their own words of sorrow so they won't feel as if they are grieving alone.

It's important that your child's needs are taken care of, even if by someone else. Also, request assistance from other adults if your own sorrow becomes overwhelming.

A Child's Needs

- Explain to the child exactly what has happened, but in terms they can understand; and on their level.

- Help them acknowledge their fears concerning a parent's death, and show them how to overcome that fear.

- Offer constant reassurance so they can understand that their parent's death wasn't their fault.

- Listen carefully to what they are trying to communicate to you.

- Realize your child is also grieving, and accept the way they are feeling.

- Do things that help them feel safe.

- Assist your child in understanding that others care how they feel.

- Remember to mention the deceased during holidays and special days so the child feels somewhat consoled following the loss.

- Continue to remember the parent who has died by mentioning them each day, and in front of the child.

- Offer to pray with the child.

"But you, O God, do see trouble and grief; you consider it to take it in hand. The victim commits himself to you; you are the helper of the **fatherless**" *(Psalms 10:14)*

"I will be a **father** to you, and you will be my sons and daughters, says the Lord Almighty" (2 Corinthians 6:18)

"He defends the cause of the **fatherless**..., giving him food and clothing" *(Deuteronomy 10:18)*

"...I rescued the poor who cried for help, and the **fatherless** who had none to assist him" *(Job 29:12)*

"A father to the **fatherless**, a defender of widows, is God in his holy dwelling" *(Psalms 68:5)*

"The Lord watches over the alien and sustains the **fatherless** and the widow..." *(Psalms 146:9*

"We have become orphans and **fatherless**, our mothers like widows" *(Lamentations 5:3)*

"Do not oppress the widow or the **fatherless**" *(Zechariah 7:10)*

Birthday

Today was my son's birthday
But he won't celebrate
It's time for one more birthday
But now it is too late

Morel birthdays will come and go
But never quite the same
The age of twenty-two
He always will remain

© *J. Hannah Lloyd*

Chapter Nineteen

When a Sibling Dies

Whether you were close to your sibling or not, if they die your sense of loss will be overwhelming.

Losing my Brother

By Austin Allen

I was in shock when I found out my brother Matt had been killed. In fact, I didn't want to think about it. I only wanted to pretend it hadn't happened.

But when I did think about it I had feelings of deep remorse. I was sorry I hadn't been a better example for him. I regretted not allowing myself a closer relationship with him. And, I felt great sadness that I would never again have another chance to do things differently.

My guilt, for the most part, has been over allowing unimportant things to take the place of quality time with him. Although I had many memories running through my head after he died, I couldn't concentrate on any one of them. I just wanted the bad news to go away.

Even to this day I live with regret over things I could have done differently with my little brother. Before he died I didn't understand what the consequences of losing him would be. But now I do.

***

Understanding a Sibling's Death

It's hard to comprehend life without someone you grew up with, shared ordinary days and unique moments with, and enjoyed holidays and vacations with. But now the reality of a sibling's death is sinking in.

Grasping the veracity that the both of you shared the same parents, the same futures, similar goals and friends can make one understand how lonely it will be. The sheer sadness of a sibling's death will also make that reality unbelievable, harsh, and unrelenting.

Realize that now is the time to let your own friends be your support as you grieve. Also, take time to seek out others who are also grieving as this will be beneficial as well as restorative. Sharing memories of the past will also bring laughter and related understanding as ways are discovered to grieve and heal from your loss.

Learn to appreciate those around you who provide needed support and understanding. Then embrace that assistance as you heal from the pain of losing your loved one. Strength from sharing will also help bring healing and restoration to heart, mind, and soul.

It's also important to remember your loved one throughout the years when dates such as their birthday occur; and recall those moments spent together. Over time, and as the heart continues to heal, more pleasant memories will surface. And, by keeping those memories alive, your loved one will remain a special part of everyday life.

Missing You

All these many new inventions
Would have had all your attentions

As things have changed so drastically
You would have loved fantastically

When only six short years ago,
You were alive and in the flow

But now those years are in the past
Yet grief and sadness seem to last

As heartache leads to sudden rage
Huge teardrops fall upon this page

I'm angry for your sudden death
For you were full of life, and breath

The things you missed, after you died
Fracture my heart so I have cried

You thought you were invincible
But death came unpredictable

Your wrong mistake became your err
Misjudgment was your final snare

© *J. Hannah Lloyd*

When one realizes a deceased sibling no longer has a future on this earth, the result will be heartbreaking. The loss of opportunity, the regret of promises made and not kept, and the useless waste of time will also be staggering as the hopelessness of reality sinks in.

But in the aftermath, sudden sadness will still overtake your senses. You may even feel shame after realizing you could have been a better brother or sister. Sorrow and sadness will then linger, and be frustrating as well as depressive.

Conflicting thoughts and emotions will also be confusing after this death. *What if things had happened differently? I can't believe he's dead. What if?*

Sadness

After the sun has set
After the day is gone
I'm left at last to think
All by myself alone

Deep sadness then engulfs me
And tears begin to flow
A storm is just beginning
And I am feeling very low

Your face then comes before me
Yet the past is all I know
But you are in my future
And I can't wait to go

For there you are so happy
Not like you were before
Quiet peace is all around you
No fighting like at war

Everything is clear and new
It is as it should be
And nothing else can matter
For you have been set free

© J. Hannah Lloyd

After the passing of a loved one, the significance of mortality can overtake the mind. The sudden ache of sorrow and the sharpness of disappointment will then surface when one realizes they will never again see their loved one alive. This emotion will be devastating.

Acute horror at death's reality—the completeness of life—will also be overwhelming. The truth of existence, as it was, has now become strange and un-real, even scary. But pondering what one could have done differently only re-ignites the grieving mechanisms all over again.

Mysteries

Mysteries I'll never know
The crash that ended your life
The pain you must have felt
On that awful, rainy night

Your troubled life near over
Were you full of anger and strife?
Your thoughts...were they on the Lord
On that awful, rainy night?

Did you realize the outcome?
Did you even try to fight?
As your life was almost over
On that awful, rainy night?

You were by yourself alone
The wrecked car held you tight
As your mind was surely racing
On that awful, rainy night

One shot into the night
Then ambulance and police alike
Arrived to give assistance
On that awful, rainy night

Emergency staff imperfect
As they tried to do things right
And worked so hard to save you
On that awful, rainy night

You then took your final breath
And stepped into the light
But left us all so empty
On that awful, rainy night

© *J. Hannah Lloyd*

Anger and remorse may set in following the demise of a loved one. But grinding memories of raw hurt and disbelief will be hard to deflect. All of a sudden you will realize you're the lone survivor, and begin to blame yourself. Feelings of guilt at being the one who's left standing can be staggering.

Survivor guilt is a common emotion, making it easy to accuse yourself. Harsh feelings of regret may then surface. Yet blaming yourself is a distorted mindset that can be damaging, and should never be considered on any level. However, these emotions may be especially true if your sibling was young, with their entire life in front of them.

Siblings, brothers and sisters, have a special type of relationship. Childhood and years spent together while growing up allows them to learn everything possible about each other. A lifetime of competition has likely strengthened that relationship.

Learning the give-and-take of life has uniquely bonded you and your sibling together. Fighting, loving, teasing, defending, and hating each other is all part of growing up together. Yet when your sibling dies, that tie is forever broken, and a part of you will always be missing.

Forgotten Survivors

Siblings of a brother or sister who has died are often the forgotten survivors. It doesn't matter the age of the one who's left. The hurt is almost always the same.

Children that remain when a sibling passes away are often overlooked by parents, friends, or other relatives in the family. Parents who are grieving for themselves often forget that their other children are also dealing with sorrow. Or, they may feel a need to protect them from the emotions of losing a sibling. But in reality, parents need to understand that the death of their child will strongly affect their remaining children.

When a sibling dies, those left behind, no matter the age, are considered secondary mourners to spouses, parents, or other children of the one who has died. However, children still living at home will take second place as the dead sibling takes prominence. He or she may then *lose* their parents for a time as they grieve the death of their deceased child.

But if the death was a suicide, the surviving siblings' role in the family may then become altered. Children often feel protective of their parents, or the parents may try to shield their living children, no matter the age, as they become fearful of also losing them. Therefore sibling survivors can easily become forgotten mourners.

People often forget the importance of a sibling in their life. But the bond between siblings during childhood is unique and special. The longest relationship in life is almost always with a sibling. Yet when one dies, extreme anxiety will surface as a result of the close relationship shared during a lifetime together. This connection is usually the longest relationship shared with anyone. And because siblings are just a few years apart in age, they will know each other longer than spouses, parents, or even their own children.

Brothers and sisters will also share more of life events and life changes with each other than with anyone else. They have the same family, the same culture, the same religious beliefs, and the same material possessions. And, as children, they will teach each other how to communicate with everyone else, and how to function in society. In fact, siblings will spend more time together in their earlier years than they will ever spend with their parents.

A child's reaction to the death of a sibling will also establish the way they will always view death. However, many fail to believe that children need to grieve, but they do. And because small children have a shorter attention span than adults, their sorrow may appear short in endurance as it only surfaces for short periods of time. Yet their grief may cause headaches and other physical problems. Children are undeveloped and may have difficulty coping with the loss of a sibling. It will also be difficult for them to know how to express their sorrow.

Children are very aware when someone close to them has died, especially if a brother or sister. Even very young children realize that death brings loss and sadness. And although small in stature, a child has feelings that need to be addressed.

But as a concerned adult, don't ignore their sentiment while trying to deal with your own. Children will go through the grieving process in much the same way as an adult.

Greatly Missed

He stepped into our lives
The time was oh so brief
At such a tender age
He left us with such grief

He died one rainy night
Rain and tears were mingled then
Lost control and lost his life
No one knows just how or when

He entered Heaven's gate
So young and yet no voice
His time had come to enter
There was no other choice

He went before we did
This was a brand new twist
This never should have happened
He will be greatly missed

© J. Hannah Lloyd

When a young child dies, the surviving children may feel abandoned. However, their need for affirmation is critical. They also need to understand that they're not themselves dying. But all these changes will be confusing if their needs aren't attended to.

Try to remember they have emotions too, and allow the child to discuss their thoughts in depth as it will lessen the severity of their hurt. Understanding what has happened will also ease their pain and make this death easier to accept.

Talk to survivors in a language they will understand and respond to. But if they're very young, use words they can comprehend. If older, use language they will identify with.

Matthew's Pond

Come on, let's go down
And visit Matthew's Pond
We'll search for hidden treasures
Inside nature's wand

We'll watch Mud Puppy's swim
While catching fish galore
And dig for unseen riches
In imagination's store

Because this world of fun
Lives deep beneath the water
He netted lots of swimmers
And tanked them all together

He loved all lakes and streams
With creatures he could tame
And so we named this pond
In honor of his name

© *J. Hannah Lloyd*

The truth of youth is doing things without considering the outcome. Having fun is the name of the game. It doesn't matter what others may say, the young will leave their mark in every corner of our world. And if they die, those corners will still be there, abandoned but waiting in silence for you.

Silence

He was good with guitar strings
A talented son was he
New lessons gave him rhythm
But gifted notes were free

At every music store and stand
He gathered guitar pics
And kept them all as treasured gifts
He boasted quite a mix

Yet his anger played right through the strings
As he strung his notes with violence
But now that room is quiet and still
And echoes from the silence

© *J. Hannah Lloyd*

Chapter Twenty

When a Friend Dies

When Lazarus died Jesus was so overcome with sorrow that he cried. There wasn't any doubt in his mind his friend would live again. And yet he couldn't stop the tears from flowing. The human side of Jesus then felt the emotional anguish of grief because someone he dearly loved had died.

Losing my Best Friend

As a child growing up in rural North Carolina with very few neighbors, I was blessed to have a friend close to my age living nearby. Bonnie lived across the street, and together we spent many happy hours.

The woods behind us was our extended playground. And when we engaged in *'Playing Indian',* our Wigwams were built from broken tree branches found throughout the wooded area. Moss growing in abundance on the forest floor was our pretend bed. And our children were treasured dolls and fuzzy kittens dressed in faded baby clothing.

Hours of imaginational play then developed as we tramped down a well-worn walking path to what we called *the Mica Mine,* a small dugout cave near our homes where the mica mineral was abundant, and spilled beyond the entrance. Then together, Bonnie and I generated many hours of treasured memories.

My Best Friend
To Bonnie

You were my best playmate
And my favorite friend
Alone we were nothing
But together we could win

Always with each other
As children we would share
Our snacks and treasured toys
And we always played with flair

Forever sharing secrets
We bonded as a twin
You were like my sister
My playmate and my friend

Dreams were for a lifetime
A motto yet unspoken
Our friendship was a pledge
And never to be broken

We'll always be as one,
My playmate and my friend
No one can separate us
Our friendship has no end

© *J. Hannah Lloyd*

In warmer weather we played in my father's corn crib, creating a cozy home-like environment for ourselves and our babies. *Hide and Go Seek, Ain't-No-Bears-Out-Tonight,* and *Rock School* were other games we played. Many hours were also spent rolling down the hill in freshly mowed grass. But as we grew, our relationship flourished, and Bonnie became the sister I never had.

And when autumn arrived we could be found playing in bales of hay stored in the barn. We also spent many formative hours pretending to be wives, mothers, and housekeepers. Even a Saturday afternoon ball game in the yard wasn't unusual, and very satisfying when played with my brother and other visiting friends.

Although climbing a steep hill near the church was tedious, it was worth the hike as we tramped through the cold snows of winter. The reward was sliding back down over frozen, icy snow in plastic washtubs and worn out sleds.

Then, as we matured, fixing hair and applying make-up became more important than favored childhood games. Boyfriends had to be considered and teenage issues discussed in detail. Sharing hopes and dreams with my best friend remains a treasured memory from my youth.

Later, when Bonnie was diagnosed with uterine cancer, she renewed her trust in God as her primary source of strength. But it was imperative she had his arm to lean on through her diagnosis, cancer therapy, and ultimate resignation to dying. The others who supported her also became a lifeline of hope until she died.

Punching the Wind

God is our refuge and strength, an ever-present help in
trouble. (*Psalms 46: 1*)

I knew life could get hard
Sometimes it left terrible wounds
But I didn't think *this* would happen

And when it did I kept asking,
"Why me?
There were no answers

Sometimes I wanted to cry out loud
I wanted to blame someone
I wanted to lash out

To scream
And wildly wave my arms
I wanted to shout, "It's just not fair!"

But that got me nowhere
That got me nothing
It was like punching the wind

And then I cried out, "Lord, help me.
Please help me through this."
And, he did

© *J. Hannah Lloyd*

There was nothing more I could do for my friend except to lend an ear and my sympathies. Although powerless to help, I knew she rested in God's hands. And that became my comfort.

But due to prior difficulties, Bonnie's delicate surgery had to be performed at Duke University Hospital in Durham, North Carolina. Then following surgery her doctor declared her cancer free.

However, and a few weeks following, complications set in which caused increasing pain. Yet her surgeon continued to insist she was cancer free although she was suffering. Later she was able to get a second opinion. Her new doctor then prescribed a pain management regimen when it was discovered she wasn't cancer free after all. But by this time her disease had spread to her lungs and liver.

She then realized her surgeon had been overconfident and somewhat arrogant in his work ethic as he refused to accept the fact her cancer hadn't completely been removed, but had spread. It would have been easier had he acknowledged his mistake and offered an apology for the mismanagement of her disease. But because of his lack of concern she wasn't re-treated in time to save her life. Although she began another regimen of chemo, the cancer was winning.

Still ashen and frail, she continued her struggle to survive. The last time I saw her alive she asked me to write her saga. And, with this narrative, I'm fulfilling her desire to have her story told.

In my eyes Bonnie was a hero. With grace and dignity she maintained her poise and composure as she battled against terminal cancer.

The Comforter Says

I will hold you in your sorrow
Give to me your grieving heart
All your strength will come from me
Peace from you will not depart

I am strong and I will keep you
Lean on me with all your might
You don't have to fear or worry
I will help you win this fight

Life has hit you fierce and hard
It's a test to bring you near
I will hold you close to me
You will no more have to fear

I am with you as you grieve
Place your lonely hand in mine
I will calm you with my peace
It's my promise for all time

© *J. Hannah Lloyd*

Bonnie spent the final months of her life re-living the triumphs of a successful marriage and the accomplishment of motherhood. But the disconcerted hurts in her life needed to be negotiated and laid to rest. Remorse and anger often surfaced as she battled numerous demons while struggling to forgive.

Then, as her sounding board, I spent many exhaustive hours listening to her grievances and concerns. During conversation she detailed unrelenting distress over terminal cancer and her impending death. Scores of narrative included comprehensive words of hope, listless expressions of despair, and later, ultimate resignation to the truth of her fate.

Although she lived with the expectation of a cure, and faith in God, she knew she may not survive her war. Still she was a fighter, and struggled to the very end as she wrestled with medicines and harsh treatments. Her family needed her and, for her, it was worth every effort taken to extend her life.

Another Time—Another Place

Another place, another time
You were always on my mind
Childhood makes for innocent rhyme
Another place, another time

Memories blocked by fewer lines
The past you think of many times
You were so sweet—you were so kind
Another place, another time

Life passes by in certain time
The years go fast and then you find
Youth far away and then you say
Another place, another way

You dream of love and then you find
Uncertainty of a different kind
Innocence gone, but love remains
Another place, but not the same

So quick you passed
Death did replace
The life you had
It was a trace

Of another time, another place

© J. Hannah Lloyd

Fifty-one is young by many standards. And yet when Bonnie realized her death was closing in on her, she conceded and began to plan her own funeral. It seemed to ease her mind as she utilized her last weeks in expectation of her final departure.

With the help of her husband and son, she chose the perfect burial plot at the cemetery. She also pre-arranged her committal at the funeral home of her choice. The church service was also planned, songs selected, and speakers chosen. Everything was designed in the minutest of detail. The pallbearers would be her son's Boy Scout troop, and her beloved horse would be saddled in a gorgeous blanket of funeral flowers in her honor. And, it was so.

The detailed serenity of the memorial service coupled with a decorative graveside interment concluded the final chapter of my best friend's life. It was a serene and beautiful ceremony conducted in honor of daughter, wife, mother, and friend—just as she had planned. Her consideration for her loved ones was accomplished in elaborate detail.

Bonnie and I shared many secrets throughout the years. Our childhood together created a unique bond between us; and our friendship continued until death took her away.

I still miss my friend.

Memories

All that's left are memories
Restored in picture form
As I sleep

Dreams of a happier past
Free from the knowledge
That life is passing me by

Unconscious and unaware
That grief exists
After all

© *J. Hannah Lloyd*

He Held My Hand, a book written by Deborah Morocco Mason, details her personal battle with cancer. Then following Bonnie's diagnosis I handed her a copy, and this book became a lifeline of hope as she battled her disease.

Before she died, she ordered copies of that same book and had them delivered to her cancer treatment facility to be shared with other cancer patients.

Her concern for others remains a legacy.

Chapter Twenty-One

Possessions

Saving a personal possession of the deceased as a token of remembrance is a wonderful way to help alleviate the pain of losing them. Family members, relatives, and friends who are given the opportunity to keep an article that once belonged to their loved one is a kind gesture for the grief stricken. Many received items following the death of a loved one are now favored heirlooms.

Memories are often attached to things that are passed down from generation to generation to later become a memorial of the departed. Great-Great-Granny's old biscuit bowl carved from a tree by Great-Great-Grandfather is a unique commemorative from the past. An antique dresser or weathered kitchen cabinet can also be incorporated into your own living space as a way of alleviating your sorrow.

Receiving an item that once belonged to the deceased will also allow feelings of closeness to remain. Retaining items for historical redemption can be another way of connecting with the past in a soothing way.

Keepsakes such as ashes in an urn placed on the mantle, or a favorite picture of the departed, can inject precious memories that help to heal the heart. An old chair, a favorite piece of clothing, or a beautiful piece of jewelry can also provide consolation to a family member. Even cards and letters will bring some aspect of closure to the pain.

***

When my son's few belongings were placed in my hands following his death, uncontrollable tears rolled down my face and splashed to the floor. But the most personal item was his wallet.

How many times had I seen him reach for it, and then return again to his back pocket? Sometimes his wallet was so full his pant pockets sagged beneath the weight. This article was his personal filing cabinet where notes, cards, and mementos were stored. Money wasn't the primary objective for this leather container, but the wallet was, without a doubt, an intricate part of his personality.

Then, with overwhelming emotion that was almost sacred, I fingered his worn wallet when handed to me. But raw sensations and a renewed realism of truth instantly boggled my mind as I realized, just hours before, this cherished piece of leather was in Matthew's back pocket next to his breathing body.

Treasures

My mansion is in heaven
Not anywhere on the earth
This treasure is forever
Just go and count the worth

With streets of purest gold,
And gates of priceless pearl
A mansion built for me
Much larger than this world

Then who would want to wait
For this world of bliss?
And who would count the cost too high
That they would want to miss?

Many people like to build
Huge mansions on this earth
While thinking that it proves
Their monetary worth

But my treasures are in heaven
Where thieves can't steal away
Where moths cannot destroy
And will be mine one day

You may want to stay
But I am ready to go
I want to see my son
And others that I know

In heaven just inside
With Jesus by the gate

I'm ready now to go
And I can hardly wait

The Bible says my heart
Is where my treasures be
So I'm going to my treasure
And spend eternity

© *J. Hannah Lloyd*

"...for where your treasure is, there your heart will be also" *(Luke 12:34)*

"Do not store up for yourselves treasures on earth, where moth and rest destroy, and where thieves break in and steal. But store up for yourselves treasures in heaven, where moth and rust do not destroy, and where thieves do not break in and steal" *(Matthew 6:19, 20)*

At some point following the death of a loved one, questions of what should be done with their personal belongings will surface. However, there's no set time to make this decision. In fact, it may take months, even years, before that issue can be addressed. But when you're ready, be prepared for renewed moments of sorrow and grief.

What treasured memento will you keep for yourself? And are you willing to share with family or friends? Perhaps you aren't prepared to let go of anything. Will you ever be? These questions, and more, will need answers at some point in the future.

But realizing others could benefit from a loved one's clothing or personal items is a step in the right direction. In fact, holding on to material things could paralyze the grieving process. And yet, when those things are shared, perhaps with those in need, your willingness to release them will also assist in releasing your loved one.

Chapter Twenty-Two

Nightmare of Reality

"**B**ut the fruit of the Spirit is love, joy, peace, patience, kindness, goodness, faithfulness, gentleness and self-control. Against such things there is no law" *(Galatians 5:22, 23)*

It was more than difficult to visit the funeral home just to see the battered, bruised, and crushed body of my youngest child with my own eyes. But it was necessary, and needed for closure. Yet because Matthew was my baby, the pain was unbelievable. And when I entered the staged room where he was, I became numb.

His body was stiff and silent, and his swollen head oozed a slow stream of blood; evidence of recent trauma. Even the metal slab where he lay was cold and rigid.

He was as he had died; not yet prepared for burial. Still I wanted to touch him, and hold him close; to cradle him and tell him how sorry I was this had happened—that he deserved better than this. I wanted to tell him how much I loved him; that past conflicts weren't important, but that he was; and that—somehow—everything would be alright.

But I didn't, and it wasn't. I just stood stone-cold in front of him; unable to move, unable to think, and unable to cry. I didn't want to believe this was my child.

His arms were lifeless, his face immobile. His eyes were closed, closed by the coroner for my viewing. His head was turned sideways, and his mouth open as if asleep. Then stepping forward, I wanted to shake his arm and tell him to get up. I wanted to lift him off that cold slab and

135

say, "What are you doing? You have your life to live. Get up and live it."

Instead I leaned over and touched his arm, and his hand; but they were cold, stiff, and lifeless—not warm and yielding. This wasn't the Matthew I'd given birth to, raised, and then released into adulthood. But it *was* him.

It was impossible to understand what my bewildered eyes were observing. In fact, this was too much to comprehend, so I put my thoughts and emotions aside to later dissect, one at a time; and then re-live each moment, second by second, minute by minute. But for now my tortured mind could not grasp the truth. These were moments best left for another time.

And there, standing beside me was Kyle, concern written all over his face. Yet on the inside we were both stunned, and dazed at the same time.

***

We confirmed our instructions with the director of the funeral home, and then drove to the home of my former in-laws where Matthew had been living. Although many years had passed, their arms opened in sympathy and understanding; and together we grieved. It was surreal.

The following day we traveled back to the funeral home with Austin. And, in disbelief, he stared, unreserved, at his brother positioned on the cold slab; his pointer finger resting on his chin. I could only imagine his thoughts.

***

The funeral service was planned for Saturday, that same week. Rick, a former brother-in-law, would officiate. Then somehow, everything fell into place as God provided ministers, a church, and everything needed for the funeral. Many locals—former friends from my first marriage not seen in years—responded to our tragedy.

Earlier that year, after Kyle's employment moved us

to Charlotte, North Carolina, we began to attend an upstart but growing church ministry. Although small in number, the possibilities of fellowship appeared strong. But when Matthew died, the founder and pastor of this small church suddenly became unavailable. It then became painfully obvious his ministry didn't include assisting the bereaved.

But God, Jesus, and the Holy Spirit traveled with us, and stood beside us through the most horrifying and traumatic moments ever experienced. In retrospect, the support of the Trinity was all that truly mattered.

When someone close to you dies it doesn't take long to find out who cares, and who doesn't. Allow the unsympathetic to walk away. Holding on to someone who is indifferent, uncaring, and heartless is simply a waste of time.

Why Me?

Oh, Lord, please help me
I know I'm falling fast
As dark is getting darker
And I'm alone at last

Who sees and understands
That I'm sinking in despair
When nothing more is right
And life seems so unfair?

But why, oh Lord, why me?
Why'd this happen to me?
My heart is crying out
And longs to be set free

I'm feeling so alone
Yet people are around
I'm drowning in despair
Yet making not a sound

© *J. Hannah Lloyd*

The church where Matthew's funeral took place was full of ex-family and friends. Several ministers were also in attendance. Many friends from my first marriage also came, offering condolences and continued prayer for our family. It was surreal.

My prayer for years was restoration of family; and salvation for Matt no matter the cost. But the family restored were my former in-laws from my abusive first marriage. *(Book-Tied to Terror-Secrets of a Battered Wife)*.

Yet God answered my prayer; not in the way I thought he would, but in the way he knew was best.

The Funeral

Strained harmony of piano and organ drifted in melodious refrain through the opened doors of the church where the funeral was to take place.

Saturday was the dreaded day—the day Matthew would be honored, and remembered. Rick, a former brother-in-law, and the pastor of a sister-church, led the family processional through wide, double doors into the sanctuary. A melancholy hush then settled over the crowd as we stumbled our way to reserved seats in the front.

But after we were seated, I glanced around the room; and my heart began to pound in explosions of disbelief. How could this be? No, this wasn't just any funeral. This was my son's funeral. I couldn't get my mind around it.

Hot tears on the verge of spilling down my cheeks were then repressed as, stoic but terrified, I faced the reality of my truth; the finality of life as it had been. This was it—the final good-bye.

Christine, Rick's wife, stood in front of a packed auditorium and began to sing *It is well with my soul*; and repressed tears then began to fall. The harmonious ebb and flow of her words, although soothing, was laborious to hear as it defined the finalization of death.

Minutes later Rick stood in front of everyone to deliver a painful eulogy over his nephew. Still I couldn't focus on his words as memories of Matt's childhood flashed before my eyes. His boyish giggles as he handed me a bouquet of wilted wild flowers—his twinkling blue eyes and tiny freckled nose—the first time I held him after nine months of feeling him move inside of me.

"A woman giving birth to a child has pain because her time has come; but when her baby is born she forgets the anguish because of her joy that a child is born into the world" *(John 16:21)*

"When you send your Spirit, they are created...

...when you take away their breath, they die and return to the dust" *(Psalms 104:30, 29)*

Breath of Life

God gave you breath
When you were born
That gave you life
That early morn

God breathed it out
And gave to you
The breath of life
When you were new

With it was given
All you would need
To live and love
And to succeed

But when you died
That lonely night
Your soul then left
And took its flight

When you excelled
With your last breath
God took it back
Into himself

—the breath of life

© *J. Hannah Lloyd*

Matthew was born at 1:02 early Monday morning, May 10, 1982. My labor began around 11:45 Sunday evening, and just before Mother's Day ended. Matt then hurried into the world following a brief labor of just forty-five minutes. Although two weeks overdue, he made up the time with a speedy delivery.

Even as a child he generated a pattern of waiting—waiting until the last minute to finish his homework, leave his play, or get dressed for school. But when he was late, he would rush, or speed up, to recover the time. Even at death he retained that same pattern.

I can't stand it. I cannot handle this.

I wanted to run away but was too numb to move. Although the service pressed forward, for me the hands of time had stopped.

***

Later, following the service, former relatives and church family came forward to extend hands of friendship, offer condolences, and share embraces of understanding and love. At that moment I felt both honored and humbled by the abundance of caring people who took the time to attend the funeral, and acknowledge our grief. Again, it was surreal.

The Memorial

A memorial was later held for Matthew at a funeral home in my home town one week following the funeral service. But since the interment was miles from where he grew up, it seemed appropriate that his memorial, and burial, be in the same town he'd spent most of his childhood.

At the chapel we conceded to the finality of Matthew's life. Although the turnout wasn't large, those in attendance were our closest friends and relatives; and perfect for closure. Pictures of Matt's life were then shared, as were other memorials. Several childhood friends also attended as did a former Sunday school teacher.

Although sad, sharing memorials with Matthew's childhood friends made his send-off even more special, and memorable.

At the Graveside

The drive from the memorial service to the cemetery was long and tedious. Although short in distance, this ride would be Matthew's last. Then following the rituals of burial, he would be laid to rest in the unyielding ground of a local cemetery.

At the cemetery our family wound its tearful way from parked cars down a trampled path to the plot where Matthew's ashes would remain. But as we began our descent, Austin asked to carry the bronzed urn that held his brother remains.

Then, with a tender hand, he gently stroked the container. Yet his gesture displayed great emotion, and remains a loving memorial to his brother. And when I saw my best friend at the gathering I was comforted.

Not one word need be spoken. Bonnie's presence alone brought a measure of restoration to my confused and grief-stricken heart. Even now, when I recall that ominous day, unbroken memories include her as she stood in silence beside my son's grave—hands folded with quiet compassion on her face.

Then, only three years later, I found myself standing in silence beside her place of burial in the same cemetery— hands folded in renewed disbelief and added sorrow.

Remember Me

Remember me
And don't forget
My eyes of blue
And even yet

My hair has tints
Of red and gold
Or none at all
When shaved to bald

Remember me
My heart is true
My words are kind
For I love you

Remember me
When you are sad
Remember me
When you are glad

Remember me
When flowers die
Remember me
But please don't cry

Remember me
When days are cold
Remember me
When you are old

Remember me
But don't be sad
For I was glad

Death Came Quickly

In your own life
To be a part

And always know
I will remain
So very near
To you each day
Within your heart

© *J. Hannah Lloyd*

Chapter Twenty-Three

Cycle of Life

People may surround you while you're sorrowful, but you're still alone. Grieving can be shared with a community, a church, an organization, a neighborhood, or with family and friends. But when it comes down to it, this is a personal issue. The emotional pain inside is real, and it's all yours. It's an ache that won't go away.

But as a resource, most churches offer grief counseling within the walls of their own facility. Pastors, Rabbis, Priests, and clerics are also prepared to offer services when asked. Schools and other public organizations also provide guidance counselors specializing in grief counseling, or other resources that may help. Doctors and medical personnel can provide similar resources for encouragement and support, if asked. Even the newspaper can be used as a resource for gathering information on grief.

The library also provides various materials, books, and other media for the grief stricken. Funeral homes and related services always keep materials and helps available for those grieving the loss of a loved one. The Internet also offers websites and services for the bereaved.

Smaller grief ministries that offer inspiration and hope are springing up everywhere. Hospice also provides resources and meet-ups for the families of those who are drying.

There's no reason to grieve alone. And, there's no shame in requesting help, if needed, for managing your sorrow.

Memories

Today he would be twenty-five
If from that crash he did survive
He would be here and still alive
If he had not gone for that drive

The graveyard holds no mystery,
For sadness follows misery.
His life is now a history
Of memories ever haunting me

I 'oft can hear his clear demand
His trumpet blasting in the band
His guitar vibrant in his hand
While laughing loudly in the stand

I long to see him here today
And celebrate just one more way
To touch and hug, and hear him say
"I understand" and "It's okay."

And yet I don't quite understand
Just why his short life had to end
It is so hard to comprehend
That life on earth is just a lend

It's just so hard...

© *J. Hannah Lloyd*

The Holy Spirit will be your Comforter. But if you don't have this consolation, perhaps it's time to ask Jesus into your heart. Only then can you feel the warmth of God's presence as though a warm blanket of compassion is covering you. The aura of the Holy Spirit will then be you help, your strength, and your comfort as you swim through the murky waters of grief.

"...my Comforter in sorrow, my heart is faint within me" *(Jeremiah 8:18)*

Following the death of my son I found comfort in composing creative poetry and prose that detailed my sorrow. Places of solace also defined my work as words of comfort consoled my heart. Paper then became my easel and the keypad my paint brush.

Writing and re-writing to exactness was an acquired skill that provided comfort during the process of grieving. Many hours were then spent perfecting words that spoke volumes to my heartache and sorrow. And, by reading my own words, I found solace for my broken heart.

The consolation of the Holy Spirit also surrounded me as I struggled through numerous days of sorrow. When insecure emotions engulfed my spirit, God's love and reassurance revealed his peace as promised in the Bible. He was with me the very moment I learned of my son's death. He was with me when I viewed him at the morgue. And he was with me during the funeral, and the long days and nights that followed. He's with me still, bringing sweet comfort that only comes from God above.

I did not go in my own strength, but with the endurance God gave. His reassurance wasn't visible, but was concrete, and solid. God's infinite peace that passes all understanding, and beyond comprehension, has long kept me stable. And although this journey of grief has been a difficult road to travel, there is a future, and a hope.

By faith I hold on to Biblical truths written in the word of God—the Bible—and soak up the unfathomable love that continues to rain down upon me, covering my heart and soul with compassion, solace, and healing. There is no better consolation than that of the Holy Spirit.

The Picture

I looked at pictures of the man
And really could not understand
That just a couple of months before
He was alive and living more

Too young to die—too young to cry
Too young to face eternity's sigh
It breaks my heart almost in two
Because his life on earth is through

And yet he had no way to know
That he would die in a month or so
Within his picture, smiling shy
Before we said our last good-bye

He was so vibrant and so young
While living life and having fun
No one knew but the Holy One
That his race with death was soon to come

And so we remember his life on earth
By viewing pictures from his birth
And travel through his life in print
So sad it's over, and is spent

© *J. Hannah Lloyd*

Although Matthew's life was short, it still was necessary, and cherished.

The Circle

Following the death of a loved one comes mourning, anguish, distress, gloom, depression, despondency, dejection, loss of hope, ache, desolation, despair, isolation, lethargy, aching, suffering, gloominess, and regret.

Time heals all wounds; or so goes the cliché. In reality, time doesn't heal every hurt. But the passing of time will make the pain easier to accept. There are some sorrows, however, that will never reach the completed stage of healing.

At times, and when least expected, deep sadness will overtake the sorrowful. Yet there's no set time for sadness, and there's no set time for healing. But when that heartache comes, it's best to go with it. Allow those ruthless emotions to sweep over your soul. Don't hold back the tears. Tears are healing.

"Thou tellest my wanderings: put thou my **tears** into thy bottle: are they not in thy book?" (*Psalms 56:8*)

Today

Today he would be
Twenty four
But he is gone
He is no more

His stay on earth
Was way too short
Tears fall like rain
Deep is the hurt

© *J. Hannah Lloyd*

A few days after Matthew was buried I visited the local Hobby Lobby looking for a tranquil place of solace. Christian music plays continually in this store, is peaceful, and provides a tranquil atmosphere where one can shop. But minutes following my arrival, the theme song from his funeral began to play; and instantly unrestrained tears spilled from my eyes and plopped down on my chest. My grief was soon out of control, and I was drowning in my own sorrow.

Still blinded by the tears, I remained in my place; unable to walk away, or to hide my sorrow. And so I allowed my tears to flow.

Although I was in the middle of the store, I thought I was alone. But the Holy Spirit was with me, comforting me with words of consolation as the song *It is well with my soul* resounded in my ears.

***

Chapter Closed

Life's chapter is closed.
The book has been written.
There is no new mystery.
No more will be hidden.

The chapters were short
To coincide with his life
No more left to happen
There'll be no more strife

His story's been told
All chapters are read
The book has been shut
No more will be said

Life's chapter is closed
On life's mystery
The story's been read—
It's now history

© *J. Hannah Lloyd*

As time begins to heal the pain of sorrow, pleasures of life—joyfulness, happiness, delight, elation, wonder, resolution, and peace—will again return to heart and soul.

"I am worn out from groaning; all night long I flood my bed with weeping and drench my couch with tears" *(Psalms 6: 6)*

"My intercessor is my friend as my eyes pour out tears to God..." *(Job 16: 20)*

"He heals the brokenhearted and binds up their wounds" *(Psalms 147:3)*

"But I will restore you to health and heal your wounds, declares the Lord" *(Jeremiah 30:17)*

It will take time to heal your wounds. But joy comes after the mourning, and peace will follow soon thereafter.

"...and the peace of God, which transcends all understanding, will guard your hearts and your minds in Christ Jesus" *(Philippians 4:7)*

Nothing will ever be the same again following the death of a loved one, no matter the circumstance. And naught can alter one minute already lived.

Emotions of today will now reflect those from the past. And whatever happens in the future will respond to the past, and be remembered. After a loved one has passed, sadness and grief will be in the undertones of everything that happens for a period of time; if not forever.

Thoughts and feelings will continue to be affected. Emotions of the past will sweep beyond and, with boldness, await you in the future. Your sadness may fade only to again surface when least expected, and then overwhelm with renewed sorrow and grief.

Just know when others no longer care, Jesus will.

***

He is Jesus

When you've just lost your best friend
And that friendship had an end
When your heart has much to mend
There is Jesus

When you're troubled with life's pain
And there's much more loss than gain
When your tears fall down like rain
There is Jesus

When you've done all that you know
But the answers are too slow
Just reach out and you will know
There is Jesus

When you've just slid hard and fell
But there's no one you can tell
When your plans all go to hell
There is Jesus

He is waiting now for you
With a love that is brand new
He will see you make it through
He is Jesus

He will take your shattered dreams
Take your plans and broken schemes
And he'll fix them by his means
He is Jesus

He will wipe away your care
Just reach out for he is there
All his love with you he'll share
He is Jesus

© *J. Hannah Lloyd*

Chapter Twenty-Four

Memories

The aroma of pizza covered in chunky toppings drifting past my nose reminds me of Matt's favorite food. Baseball caps, his favorite piece of clothing, are now scrutinized as I wonder which one he would choose if shopping.

Every young man I see with a shaven head now reminds me of my son. He was his own barber and never failed to leave a sink full of scraggly strands for me to complain about. Today I would love to scoop them all up in my hands. Once he displayed a head full of blue hair. His bold choice of color created a huge sensation at school, and with his peers. But the embarrassment I then felt I now regret.

***

It will take time to sort through your memories. Anything and everything will now cause thoughts and reflections to surface; at least for a time. The struggle to survive those moments will be difficult at first. But once the funeral is past, they will be even more restrictive, and overwhelming.

However, during the initial stages of grieving, allow those moments of sorrow to occur. Don't disengage from them as they are essential for healing and restoration. It will take time to lift the heaviness of sorrow. But realize, you're not alone. Others are grieving with you, and also feel the same pain you're feeling. This hurt is almost always the same.

Heavy Heart

If you could know
Just how I feel
Although you're gone
You are still real

If you could touch
My heavy heart
And know my pain
From end to start

If you will hold
Eternity
I'll be there soon
Just wait for me

© *J. Hannah Lloyd*

God knows how it feels to lose a child. He also lost one—His only son—through death. What greater example is there?

Many thoughts raced through my mind the day I learned of my son's death; the sweetness of his childhood, music vibrating from his guitar as he strummed the strings; a newborn baby in my arms. But with his passing I was both perplexed and distraught at the same time. Where would I find the strength to endure what was now before me? God had willing allowed his son to die. But was I ready to release mine? I couldn't understand the logic.

Many years had been spent raising Matthew; caring for scraped knees, broken bones, and stitched cuts while loving him through it all. But those moments were dimmed in light of the heartbreak I now faced.

Although many years had passed, many hurts remained—twelve years of an abusive first marriage, a painful divorce, and the abrasive struggle of raising three children as single parent on a limited income. Even a wonderful second marriage had its own set of problems. But burying my youngest was more difficult than all the suffering I'd already endured; including a painful childhood.

Hadn't I suffered enough? My son's death was more than I could bear. But I had to trust in God. There is no one else.

"Surely God is my salvation; I will trust and not be afraid. The Lord, the Lord, is my strength and my song; he has become my salvation" *(Isaiah 12:2)*

J. Hannah Lloyd

I Think of You

I think of you when I see

Fish in aquariums
Red Toyota cars
Guitars of all kinds
Jalapenos in a jar

Blue plaid shirts
Worn Reebok shoes
Papa John's Pizza
Animals at the zoo

Rivers, lakes, and oceans
Water flooded streams,
Critters in the wild
You—laughing in my dreams

I think of you when I see

Young men everywhere
Heads shaved like a dime
Running up the stairs
Taking two at a time

A black Nissan Maxima
Like your first car
Young boys on skateboards
Kit-Kat candy bars

Music playing loudly
A funny TV show
Hearty, roaring laughter
Backyard Wiffle ball

DEATH CAME QUICKLY

The list goes on and on
Of all the things I see
That makes me think of you
And it always shatters me

© *J. Hannah Lloyd*

Matthew was an interesting artist. As a child he always scribbled on paper. But now the pieces that survived childhood give insight to his artistic abilities. Yet the world will never know his forte, for his brilliance will never be realized, or celebrated.

He also loved wildlife although fish, frogs, turtles, lizards, and other amphibians were his favorite. It was also expected he would later study to be a scientist or biologist. But when he grew up those plans were squashed as peer pressure drove him to the dark side. Still there was hope he would change direction and pursue a more productive lifestyle. But then he died, and those dreams were forever crushed. The difficulty of accepting these terms has been an absolute struggle.

As an avid reader, Matthew gained extensive wisdom by reading encyclopedias and watching scientific media. With a higher than average IQ, tested, his range of knowledge surpassed many of his peers. But a common sense factor was also missing. My explanation for his lack was simply that he would cross the road and then look to see if it was safe to do so. The clinical response would now be a diagnosis of Asperger's Syndrome, which is a high-functioning autism.

Later, as a young man, his desire to play the guitar surfaced. Then, after a few lessons, his exceptional talents were revealed. He also wanted to own unique guitars and, over time, owned several. Every music store in his path gave reason enough to visit, sample, and strum to heart's content.

Reflecting back on happier times allows positive memories to help alleviate the pressures of grieving.

When I write poetry, or short stories, I realize Matthew's life was not in vain. The wonderful incidents that occurred when he was alive are worth repeating, and provide excellent fodder for journaling. And, in this way, I can remember the past in positive ways.

Sharing memories as a family also brings healing and wholeness as it provides needed support even though the circle is now broken. But when grieving becomes critical, I try to focus on different things.

For others still grieving, learn to be selective with the memories that are worth retaining, and dwell on those. Or change your thought pattern when contemplating a downturn to despair. Reflect on joyful moments from the past and allow God to be your source of strength. (*Psalms 46:3)*

Learn to prepare for sorrowful moments with alternative reflections as decisive efforts will defray unstable thoughts.

Wounds

Life's wounds take time to heal
Yet grief is all I feel

God did not choose to kill
But my heart is broken still

Yet the future will reveal
All was in God's will

© *J. Hannah Lloyd*

"My life is consumed by anguish and my years by groaning; my strength fails because of my affliction, and my bones grow weak" *(Exodus 15:2-4)*

"The Lord is my strength and my song..." *(Psalms 118: 14)*

"God is our refuge and strength, an ever-present help in trouble" *(Psalms 46: 1)*

"Do not grieve, for the joy of the Lord is your strength" *(Nehemiah 8: 10)*

Death Came

Investments made
But for naught
Because death came
And took the lot

Removed life's plans
With the stories
Left the memories
Of life's glories

Gone in a flash.
Wind swept away
Leaving behind
Life's longest day

Where did you go?
Before my eyes blinked
When your heartbeat stopped
As death at you winked?

And who would believe
That life was a lend
'Till death took it over
And it had to end?

© *J. Hannah Lloyd*

At his death Matthew was employed, saving for college tuition, and registered to attend in the fall. The car he was driving was his own, and insured. He was also attending church on a regular basis.

Day after Day

Day after day
Week after week
Month after month
Grief after grief

Sadness and tears
Sorrow on sorrow
Grief overtakes me
Like no tomorrow

It never ends
This emptiness inside
Unexpected tears
Without reason or rhyme

Sorrow upon sorrow
And grief upon grief
Day after day
And week after week

Month after month
And year after year
Yet life goes on
And always a tear

It never ends
This grief in my heart
It's hard to believe
We both had to part

© *J. Hannah Lloyd*

There is Hope

"This is what the Lord says: "A voice is heard in Ramah, mourning and great weeping, Rachel weeping for her children and refusing to be comforted, because her children are no more."

"This is what the Lord says: "Restrain your voice from weeping and your eyes from tears, for your work will be rewarded," declares the Lord. "They will return from the land of the enemy. So there is hope for your future," declares the Lord. "Your children will return to their own land." *(Jeremiah 31:15–17)*

"Is not Ephraim (Matthew) my dear son, the child in whom I delight? Though I often speak against him, I still remember him. Therefore my heart yearns for him; I have great compassion for him," declares the Lord...." *(Jeremiah 31:20)*

"He will wipe every tear from their eyes. There will be no more death or mourning or crying or pain, for the old order of things has passed away" *(Revelation 2:14)*

A New Direction

What better way to grieve than to recall all the good times shared with a loved one before they passed? Memories can also help to sort through a loss in positive ways. But when you realize time spent with your loved is forever gone, feelings of sadness may become overwhelming. However, when this happens, re-direct your thoughts to happier moments, and hold them close to your heart.

Joining others on the Internet through Facebook and other websites is the rage for sharing words of comfort while remembering a loved one. Reading written expressions from others who are also grieving will be remedial. And although it may take years to sort through the heartache of sorrow, having a place to remember a loved one can be therapeutic, as missing them often takes center stage at unrehearsed moments.

Birthdays and anniversaries of the deceased are also occasions when raw emotions will surface. But recapturing happier moments while sifting through the rawness of grief can be curative. Comforting words in written form can also bring remedial restoration as you celebrate your loved one's life in this way.

Winter Snow

Dedicated to my children—the inspiration

Winter snowing
Faces glowing
Wind is breezing
Snowflakes teasing

Shedders sledding
Noses freezing
Snowballs rolling
Snowmen growing

Time now fleeting
Daylight leaving
Inside alluring
Cider brewing

Fire is burning
Popcorn popping
Day's not over
Snow still calling

© *J. Hannah Lloyd*

Delayed Memories

Matthew loved to play outdoors and spent much of his childhood in the various elements of rain, snow, and sun. Many hours were also spent on a rope swing while playing with his siblings. Toy trucks were also utilized as moments of sandy construction generated positive reinforcement for lengthy friendships. Neighborhood playmates were always welcomed—the more the merrier.

J. Hannah Lloyd

Sunday Afternoon Ballgame

While folks are napping
The kids are whacking
The ball goes flying
The dogs are yapping

The scores are flashing
The teams are gasping
The game is going
Our team is winning
The sport—never ending

The leaves are falling
And mom is calling
The day is ending
Fun just beginning

Friends are giving
And life is living
But never forgetting
Sunday afternoon ballgames

In my head always spinning

© *J. Hannah Lloyd*

Matthew also spent many hours during childhood with his brother and neighborhood friends playing wiffle ball, football, and sledding in the backyard; whatever the season dictated. Summertime was also made for hosing friends with a water hose when the sweltering heat required it. Even outdoor games such as hiding from siblings and friends proved to be constructive exercise. The wooded area beyond the yard also gave protection while carrying toy guns and rifles to stave off pretend enemies.

The exuberance of childhood, full of laughter and energy, emerged as pleasurable memories for all who were friends with Matthew.

But observing my children at play is forever etched in my mind, and worth taking time to recollect. Peaceful moments when life was active are best preserved in pictures and journals, and valuable solace when feelings of sadness overwhelm.

The Swing

The rope swing is empty
And sits all alone,
Just waiting for you
To come on back home

As wind blows it softly
It spins, and it turns
Still waiting for you
As autumn leaves burn

The tree is now barren
As fall turns to cold
A lonesome swing waits
For your hands to hold

Stormy winter is harsh
As a blue 'Norther blows
And snow hides the swing
As time slowly goes

Warmer days gush springtime
As mockingbirds fly by
But you're no longer here
Sailing high to the sky

Even in the summer
When everything is bright
There's no joy or laughter
As dusk turns into night

That swing was your treasure
But now it sits there quiet

© *J. Hannah Lloyd*

Chapter Twenty-Five

Grieving the Loss of a Pet

Freddie the cat was Matt's personal pet. But after his death that cat became very important to me.

Freddie seemed to understand my sadness as he stayed close beside me when my grieving became critical and out of control. Four years later he disappeared, and never returned. However, his disappearance created a new grieving pattern as his absence brought renewed feelings of sorrow.

Later, after searching the neighborhood door-to-door with pictures and posters, I discovered that several pet owners were also missing their small pets; cats as well as dogs. Later it was confirmed coyotes had been seen in the woods nearby.

Although many years have now passed since Freddie's disappearance, I continue to miss him. I've also learned that grieving the loss of a pet can be as consuming as mourning the death of a human being.

There will always be something to regenerate new pain and hurt caused by the loss of someone, or something, you've loved and cherished. It may be difficult to get beyond the sorrow as often the heart won't cooperate. But there are times it may be necessary to put your true feelings aside as other concerns challenge the issues of grieving.

But when reflections of sorrow become too raw, redeem the time by pondering them at a later time. As Scarlett O'Hara once said, "I'll think about it tomorrow."

Personal Pain

Sometimes I feel so lost
There seems to be no gain
As days and weeks go by
There's nothing's left but pain

His cat at the door
Wanting to come in
Brings back memories
Reminding me of him

However strange it is
There's comfort in his cat
As he gently rubs my face
He's saying "I know that"

Someone had to ask
If I am okay
"Just some personal pain"
Is all that I could say?

A 'smiley face' appears
As I go about my day
But tears are only hiding
And just won't go away

© *J. Hannah Lloyd*

Chapter Twenty-Six

More Reasons to Grieve

It's heart-renting for a parent to lose a child to drugs, alcohol, prostitution, or other influences in this world. It's also difficult to stand back and watch as a child disregards, and then discards parental love and positive training without a second thought.

But when that child is of age there's nothing more you can do, as a parent, to prevent them from making immoral choices and wrong decisions. Just pray for them, entrust their life to God, and believe that one day they will return home.

Bring Them Home

By Cindy Sproles

"Your children hasten back... Lift up your eyes and look around; all your children gather and come to you. As surely as I live," declares the Lord, "you will wear them all as ornaments; you will put them on, like a bride" (*Isaiah 49:17-18*)

Sometimes we do for the good of the many at the cost of the one—even when that decision crushes our hearts.

My husband tightened the last screw into the lock.

"This is our home," he said. "We shouldn't have to put locks on our door." He dropped the screwdriver back into his tool box and walked into our son's room.

"Box up his stuff. All of it. He's got to hit bottom before he'll change."

That night every item I packed away was bathed in tears. Our child, lost. We had to push him away, turn our backs for a time, and pray that God would restore him.

Five years passed, two without any word, any news, or any knowledge. The rest were sporadic sightings of him from a distance. Shoving him away was the hardest thing we'd ever done; the sacrifice of the one for the health and safety of the rest of our family.

God moved away from His children for a time, too. They had to hit bottom in order to be restored. Renovation isn't a pretty process. Walls are ripped down, wires uncrossed, foundations repaired. But God promised to refurbish, build up, and repair. He promised to bring our children, and his, back; to gather them around us.

I prayed every morning this year that God would restore my family. *Bring our prodigal home to the arms of the parents who love him.* As Christmas approached, we heard he was on his way. But we'd heard this before and he was always a no-show. Would he *no-show* again?

Christmas arrived. Our door opened and there was our prodigal. Home. I gazed across the room at our four sons laughing together as though no time had passed. Not only had God restored our family, but He'd wiped away the hurt of memories past. Our home was filled with joy; and when the evening ended, I took a picture of our boys, gathered together, and placed it near my heart. *"You will wear them all as ornaments."*

God is a God of restoration. He understands tough love and the pain it demands. But He delights in restoring your soul. Have you felt the sting of loss? What treasured relationship needs to be restored in the New Year? Let the Master Carpenter do his job.

***

Additional reasons to grieve

- Losing a job that defined you for years

- Moving away from family and friends

- Trusting a friend who later betrayed you

- An injury or disease that changed your relationship with someone you loved

- Losing your home

- Trusting someone who later proved to be untrustworthy

- Bad health

- Sickness unto death

- Losing hope-depression

- Divorce

Chapter Twenty-Seven

Grief Recovery

A loved one's death may have been unexpected as caused by an accident or sudden illness. Or perhaps their demise was expected. But whether expected or not, the startling shock of that event will be disturbing. However, it's important to find someone to talk with that understands your sorrow. The best assistance for grief recovery is to share the pain with others. Family and friends may be your best resource. But remember. You don't have to travel this road alone.

Don't be afraid to ask for help from clergy, or from medical professionals either. Take advantage of this time to recover with tools that will benefit you for the rest of your life. It could be an investment that saves your sanity.

Also resist the urge to lock yourself away and grieve alone. The world is full of grieving people. Sharing your distress with others will help to reduce feelings of sadness. In return their support can convey comfort with words and actions of encouragement. Again remember—there will always be someone who cares.

Many outlets are now available that encourage discussions and forums on how to grieve. But for those who've already traveled this road of sorrow, your willingness to reach out to others is a wonderful avenue of generosity. Your readiness to assist others through their journey of grief will be embraced, and appreciated beyond measure. And because you've experienced sorrow, your approach to heart-renewal could be the only way another will recover.

Every Day

I miss him every single day
I miss him every kind of way
That pieces of my heart just break
Sometimes it's more than I can take

I miss him when the cars I see
Remind me of his driving spree
I miss him when he would rush in
Leaving doors to slam right behind him

I miss his silly kind of grin
When I was looking right at him
I miss him for his memory string
For he remembered everything

I miss him when the sad songs play
I wish this hurt would go away
I miss him calling "Hello....Hello,"
Sometimes fast, and sometimes slow

I miss him when the family meets
For he's not here—it makes me weep
I miss his style of clothes and hair
I miss his silly underwear

But now that he has gone away
I miss him more than I can say

© J. Hannah Lloyd

"For I am the Lord, your God, who takes hold of your right hand and says to you, "Do not fear; I will help you" *(Isaiah 41:13)*

"So do not fear, for I am with you; do not be dismayed, for I am your God. I will strengthen you and help you; I will uphold you with my righteous right hand" *(Isaiah 41:10)*

"Be strong and courageous. Do not be afraid or terrified..., for the Lord your God goes with you; he will never leave you nor forsake you" *(Deuteronomy 31:6)*

Chapter Twenty-Eight

Living Without

Following the loss of a loved one, coping mechanisms essential for survival can also be relevant to others in similar situations.

Matthew

More than ten years have passed since Matthew was killed. And yet there are times when sorrow is still brutally harsh. It still rips through my heart, and shreds it to pieces. And it still feels as if I've just learned of his death. Pangs of anguish still surface, and fill my heart with grief.

But there's also peace in knowing that God is in control beyond everything that has happened, and will happen. And the peace that passes all understanding still keeps me grounded, and from losing my mind when my focus becomes distorted, and sadness again claims every waking moment.

Matthew is still missed, still important, and still wanted. We still talk about him, think about him, and love him. He is still my child, Samantha's uncle, Haley and Austin's brother, and a friend of many. He is, and always will be, a special part of everyday living.

When all is said and done, I'm still blessed to have been his mother, and given the opportunity to enjoy his life as it unfolded before me. He is, and always will be, a light in the darkness of this world.

Dominic

By Cathy Pendola

It has been nine years since I lost my precious son Dominic in a car accident. I still feel like I'm talking about someone else when I say that, because it is surreal to me that he is gone. As a parent you feel like your prayers are a wall of protection around your child that nothing can permeate. It's a shock to find out that the control you thought you had was just an illusion.

Time does pad your heart and give you some perspective, but I believe when you lose a child, a part of you walks away and never comes back. You learn how to live again, but the landscape of your life is forever changed. I think about Dom every, single day and I will until the day I die because he was my son, and I loved him; and it is my privilege to do so. My heart goes out to anyone who has lost a child.

Here is what I've learned, and what I know:

1. Just say, "I'm sorry for your loss." You can't fix it.
2. It's okay to talk about my child. I need to hear Dominic's name spoken. Don't be upset if I cry.
3. If someone asks me how many children I have, I will tell them I have a daughter and a son.
4. Reach out to someone who is hurting. It is healing.
5. There will always be moments that break your heart.
6. You never get over it. There is no answer to "why," but you search for it.
7. Breathe. Put one foot in front of the other. Don't let anyone tell you how to grieve.

You can swim against the riptide of grief until you're exhausted, but eventually you have to learn to roll on your back and float with the current of life. I'm a strong swimmer, but I am learning to float. Each day is an opportunity for me to embrace life and I want to do this to honor Dom's life. I know he walks with me; I can feel it. There is hope and there is light. I've learned to never miss an opportunity to say 'I love you.'

Living by Faith

By Belle Woods

Widowhood has been an adventure at times and a mystery at other times. It has been nearly seven years since my sweet Danny left to be with the Lord. So much happened in the first six months after.

Danny had life insurance on the mortgage, but when we refinanced, the loan officer had all the paperwork ready and waiting for him to sign. She slid the papers across the desk and told him to sign on the x's. But I couldn't sign any of the papers because he was the only one with income.

The following week after his funeral I talked to my personal banker to get the paperwork process started for the mortgage insurance. She began the paper work and then suddenly said, "Oh no!" Of course I was wanting to know what. She began to explain to me that the paperwork he had signed stated that he wasn't on disability on one page and on another he signed for it to be withdrawn from his disability payment. She then told me the insurance may not pay out. Fear wanted to overtake me. But without the mortgage being paid off, I couldn't live in the home we had owned for almost 15 years. I knew I had to trust in my God.

My banker decided to go ahead and submit the claim. She said, "I hope you believe in prayer", to which I wholeheartedly replied, "Yes". So now began the trial of faith, and the waiting game.

We also had a small equity loan of about sixteen hundred dollars. Well, it was in Danny's name only. They could not give me any information on the loan, but yet the main bank in Los Angeles began calling me and telling me that if I didn't pay it off, they could and would take my home! I asked for information so I could pay on it but was told they could not give me that information because of the privacy laws. "What do I do Lord?" Quietly and peacefully I heard, "Talk to an attorney and wait on Me."

I still continued to make the payments on the mortgage every month. But the only income I had was from the kindness of my church family and friends. On that money I continued to tithe, just as my husband and I had done since we became engaged.

The attorney I contacted was very understanding and helpful. He was also very angry at how the bank was treating me with constant phone calls every few days and asking me to do what was impossible. He wrote a letter to the bank and sent a copy of Danny's death certificate and that they were to release the information so I could take over the account. In a week I got a call, and an apology, from one of the CEO's who helped get everything set up so I could begin to pay off the equity loan. Plus the attorney handled it Pro-Bono. God is so faithful!

Three months after Danny left, I received a phone call from my personal banker. She asked if I was sitting down. After telling her that I was and thinking this was not good, she told me that the insurance had paid off my home! I started praising the Lord and shouting! My God who promised He would be a Husband to the Widow was doing just that.

Six months later I was approved to receive Danny's Social Security, but only about eighteen hundred dollars came in, of which, as I said before I tithed off of. But during that time, not one bill went unpaid, not one need went unmet. I look back on that now and wonder how did He do it? For my daughter and me to live on that for six months is nothing short of a miracle. Plus, after the insurance paid off the mortgage the bank put all three of the payments I made back into my account. Praise the Lord!

If you are a widow, whether it has been a while or just recently. I encourage you to "Trust in the Lord with all your heart and lean not to your own understanding. In all your ways acknowledge Him and He will direct your paths" (Proverbs 3:5-6)

Life is different without my husband, but I have peace, joy and comfort in my Lord and Savior Jesus Christ.

Just be my Friend

Just grieve with me
And understand
The pain in my heart
Just be my friend

Just cry with me
And hold my hand
And feel my hurt
Just be my friend

Just be with me
And help me mend
And let me talk
Just be my friend

Just pray with me
'Till I can stand
Just be with me
Just be my friend

© *J. Hannah Lloyd*

Chapter Twenty-Nine

Reflection and Resolution

Reflection

One day I noticed a bird flying too low in front of a speeding car. Then, as I watched, the car whizzed past and the bird fell with a thud to the road. But when it didn't move from its place, I knew it was dead.

After a short moment, another bird flew to its side and stood for a long time; watching in silence as if grieving. But the second bird's actions instantly brought tears to my eyes as its sorrow was reflected. Later it flew away to never again return. Yet somehow that bird knew its mate was dead.

The Missing Part

A part of me is missing
Of flesh and blood and life
My loved one I'm still grieving
He died alone one night

© *J. Hannah Lloyd*

If God sees a sparrow fall, how much more does he care when one of his own, his greatest creation, falls from this life?

J. HANNAH LLOYD

"... how much more valuable you are than birds"
(Luke 12:24)

Who Knows

Who knows?
The pain of cruel grief
A hollow broken heart
Facing uncertain days
As lives are ripped apart

Who knows?
Regret and raw despair
While trying to endure
The nights so long
When nothing seems secure

Who knows?
As guilt replaces reason
Day and night
Becoming one
Season after season

Who knows?
How harsh and how intense
And who knows for how long
This heartache has to last

Who knows?
And who can understand
A life that is gone—
More than losing one's best friend

Who knows?
God knows

© *J. Hannah Lloyd*

Reflection

If a time of solace is needed to reflect on past memories, or to consider the future, a visit to the cemetery may be the key. However, that stop-over can also be grueling.

When I gaze at my son's grave marker through tears of sadness, I continue to mourn his death while considering all unfulfilled hopes, dreams, and desires that will never be realized. Those quiet moments also bring a sense of closure, although upsetting at best.

Pulling stray weeds that spring up around his grave marker also provides a sense of purpose. Then leaving seasonal flowers allows the nurturing part of motherhood to surface as I continue to care for the needs of my son. But most of the time I leave in tears and a renewed broken heart.

My friend Bonnie is also buried in a plot near Matthew. Often I place a flower on her remains as a memorial to our friendship.

Visiting places a loved one enjoyed, and doing the things they liked to do, can also help to alleviate some of your sorrow. Completing an unfinished project for them may also bring a sense of closure. Even sharing memories of mutual interests with relatives and close friends is restorative.

When I drag out videos from Matthew's childhood, my mind is again soothed as, once again, I'm able to watch him laughing while engaged in joyful play. But other times the sadness is overwhelming as I realize those days are forever gone.

***

Resolution

God doesn't play fair with those he loves concerning his promises. We don't understand why God operates the way he does. And, we don't understand what's just around the corner. But God does. There is, however, a spiritual covering over a household of faith. God's promises are true. If he promised to save a household, then those members will be saved.

"The jailer called for lights, rushed in and fell trembling before Paul and Silas. He then brought them out and asked, "Sirs, what must I do **to be saved**?" They replied, "Believe in the Lord Jesus, and **you will be saved—you and your household**.

One of the criminals who hung there (on a cross next to Jesus) hurled insults at him: "Aren't you the Christ? Save yourself and us!" But the other criminal rebuked him. "Don't you fear God," he said, "since you are under the same sentence? We are punished justly, for we are getting what our deeds deserve. But this man has done nothing wrong." Then he said, "**Jesus, remember me** when you come into your kingdom." *(Acts 16: 29-31)*

Jesus answered him, "I tell you the truth, **today you will be with me in paradise**" *(Luke 23:39-43)*

Even on a deathbed the spoken name of Jesus will allow the dying to receive salvation. Believe that Jesus died on a cross, shed his blood for the atonement of sin, and returned from the dead to give life to all mankind. Faith is all that's needed to receive salvation and forgiveness. To understand is to believe.

"Jesus said to the woman, "Your faith has saved you; go in peace" *(Luke 7:50)*

"We are confident, I say, and willing rather to be absent from the body, and to be present with the Lord" *(2 Corinthians 5:8)*

***

In my heart I needed to make a critical but spiritual decision when my son Matthew died. Would I place blame on God for his death and travel down the road many had taken before me? Or would I continue to trust in the God of my salvation?

When I released my son to God it was before he was born, and again when he was having difficulty as a young man. Matthew had always been in the hands of God. I also knew there was nothing I could do that would change his destiny. But God could.

Perhaps if things had been different, or if Jeremy, his biological father, had invested time with him, this would never have happened. But instead of blaming others, I laid the blame aside, and continued to trust.

God is often blamed when a catastrophe, or unexpected death, occurs. But is it fair to reprimand the only one who understands and knows all things? He may have allowed a loved one to die a premature death just to secure their place in heaven. Or perhaps the point of death was the only time a loved one's heart would be tender enough for them to accept salvation.

There are times when the early death of a loved one is the turning point for someone else. So who are we to judge the sovereignty of God? He alone knows the end from the beginning.

"Therefore judge nothing before the appointed time; wait till the Lord comes. He will bring to light what is hidden in darkness and will expose the motives of men's hearts" *(1 Corinthians 4:5)*

God did everything possible to purchase our salvation. He even allowed his son to die in agony for the sin of the world. Why not believe he would also do whatever's necessary to honor the prayers of parents, siblings, relatives, friends, and church members who prayed in absolute faith for the salvation of a loved one?

"...he (God) hears the prayer of the righteous" *(1 Chronicles 16:11)*

"The righteous cry out, and the Lord hears them; he delivers them from all their troubles" *(Psalms 34:17)*

"...at the very time God had promised... *(Genesis 21: 2)* "Record my misery; list my tears on your scroll—are they not in your record?" *(Psalms 56:8)*

"You have collected my tears in your bottle. You have recorded each one in your book. ... You have kept count of my tossings; and put my tears in your bottle" *(Psalms 56:8) (NLT)*

***

Overcome by an unrelenting need to offer prayers of intercession for Matthew, I knelt before God one Wednesday night a few days before he died. Words for his salvation and safety then flowed from my lips as my tears flooded the Alter where I bowed. So deep was my prayer, my heart felt as if it would burst.

In retrospect, there was a reason and a purpose. A few days later he was dead.

Just as Jesus prayed in the garden before his death—

"...Going a little farther, he fell with his face to the ground and prayed, "My Father, if it is possible, may this cup be taken from me. Yet not as I will, but as you will" *(Matthew 26:39)*

God knew what was ahead for Matthew just as he knows what's ahead for us.

"For I know the plans I have for you," declares the Lord..." *(Jeremiah 29:11)*

Chapter Thirty

Bible Verses of Comfort

"**E**ven though I walk through the valley of the shadow of death, (or through the darkest valley) I will fear no evil, for you are with me; your rod and your staff, they **comfort** me" *(Psalms 23:4)*

"When I was in **distress,** I sought the Lord; at night I stretched out untiring hands and my soul refused to be comforted" *(Psalms 77:2)*

"...as a mother **comforts** her child, so will I **comfort** you; and you will be **comforted**..." *(Isaiah 66:13)*

"Do not let your hearts be troubled. Trust in God; trust also in me" *(John 14:1)*

"...who **comforts** us in all our troubles, so that we can **comfort** those in any trouble with the **comfort** we ourselves have received from God. For just as the sufferings of Christ flow over into our lives, so also through Christ our **comfort** overflows" *(2 Corinthians 1:4, 5)*

"Blessed are those who mourn, for they will be comforted" *(Matthew 5:4)*

"Ask and you will receive...." *(John 16:24)*

"Praise be to the God and Father of our Lord Jesus Christ, the Father of compassion and the God of all **comfort** who **comforts** us in all our troubles" *(2 Corinthians 1:3)*

"...and the **peace** of God, which transcends all understanding, will guard your hearts and your minds in Christ Jesus" *(Philippians 4: 7)*

"You will go out in joy and be led forth in **peace**; the

mountains and hills will burst into song before you, and all the trees of the field will clap their hands" *(Isaiah 55: 12)*

"**Peace** I leave with you; my **peace** I give you. I do not give to you as the world gives. Do not let your hearts be troubled and do not be afraid" *(John 14: 27)*

"He himself bore our sins in his body on the tree, so that we might die to sins and live for righteousness; by his wounds you have been **healed**" *(I Peter 2: 24)*

"Indeed, in our hearts we felt the sentence of **death**. But this happened that we might not rely on ourselves but on God, who raises the dead" *(2 Corinthians 1:9)*

"May the **God of hope** fill you with all joy and **peace** as you trust in him, so that you may overflow with **hope** by the power of the Holy Spirit" *(Romans 15: 13)*

"Then he said, Jesus, **remember me** when you come into your kingdom *(Luke 23:43)*

"Jesus answered him, "I tell you the truth, today you will be with me in **paradise**" *(Luke 23:42)*

"Listen, I tell you a mystery: We will not all sleep, but we will all be changed—in a flash, in the twinkling of an eye, at the last trumpet. For the trumpet will sound, the dead will be raised imperishable, and we will be changed. For the perishable must clothe itself with the imperishable and the mortal with immortality. When the perishable has been clothed with the imperishable, and the mortal with immortality, then the saying that is written will come true: "**Death has been swallowed up in victory**" *(1 Corinthians 15:5-54)*

"Where, O **death**, is your victory? Where, O **death**, is your sting?" *(1 Corinthians 15:55)*

"Marvel not at this: for the hour is coming, in the which all that are in the graves shall hear his voice, and shall come forth..." (John 5: 28, 29)

"For the Lord himself shall descend from heaven with a shout, with the voice of the archangel, and with the trump of God: and the **dead** in Christ shall rise first..." (1 Thessalonians 4:16)

"I will give them comfort and joy instead of sorrow." *(Jeremiah 31:1*

Cremation

Since cremation is often controversial, the Bible is the first place one should turn to find a resolution to that debate. Then, if one choses to go that route, there should be no condemnation.

"When the people of Jabesh Gilead heard of what the Philistines had done to Saul, all their valiant men journeyed through the night to Beth Shan. They took down the **bodies** of Saul and his sons from the wall of Beth Shan and went to Jabesh, where **they burned them.** Then they took their bones and buried them under a tamarisk tree at Jabesh, and they fasted seven day" *(I Samuel 31:11)*

Note: Because the fire wasn't hot enough to cremate bones, they were later buried.

"All go to the same place; all come from dust, and to dust all return" *(Ecclesiastes 3:20)*

Salvation and Healing

"Heal me, O LORD, and I will be **healed**; save me and I will be **saved**, for you are the one I praise" *(Jeremiah 17:14)*
"Jesus turned and saw her. "Take heart, daughter," he said, "your faith has **healed** you." And the woman was **healed** from that moment" *(Matthew 9:22)*
"The grass **withers** and the flowers **fall**, but the word of our God stands forever" *(Isaiah 40:8)*
"In this you greatly rejoice, though now for a little while you may have had to suffer **grief** in all kinds of trials. These have come so that your faith-of greater worth than gold, which perishes even though refined by fire-may be proved genuine and may result in praise, glory and honor when Jesus Christ is revealed" *(I Peter 1:6,7)*

"For none of us lives to himself alone and none of us **dies** to himself alone. If we live, we live to the Lord; and if we **die**, we **die** to the Lord. So, whether we live or **die**, we belong to the Lord" *(Romans 14: 7-8)*

"My dear children, I write this to you so that you will not sin. But if anybody does sin, we have one who speaks to the Father in our defense—Jesus Christ, the Righteous One. He is the atoning sacrifice for our sins, and not only for ours but also for the sins of the whole world" *(1 John 2:1-2)*

"For he says, "In the time of my favor I heard you, and in the day of salvation **I helped you**." I tell you, now is the time of God's favor, now is the day of salvation" *(2 Corinthians 6: 1, 2)*

"Whoever dwells in the shelter of the Most High will rest in the shadow of the Almighty" *(Psalms 91:1)*

Faith, Hope, and Love

"If I speak in the tongues of men and of angels, but have not **love**, I am only a resounding gong or a clanging cymbal. If I have the gift of prophecy and can fathom all mysteries and all knowledge, and if I have a **faith** that can move mountains, but have not **love**, I am nothing. If I give all I possess to the poor and surrender my body to the flames, but have not **love**, I gain nothing

Love is patient, **love** is kind. It does not envy, it does not boast, it is not proud. It is not rude, it is not self-seeking, it is not easily angered, and it keeps no record of wrongs. **Love** does not delight in evil but rejoices with the truth. It always protects, always trusts, always **hope**s, and always perseveres.

Love never fails. But where there are prophecies, they will cease; where there are tongues, they will be stilled; where there is knowledge, it will pass away. For we know in part and we prophesy in part, but when perfection comes, the imperfect disappears.

When I was a child, I talked like a child, I thought like a child, I reasoned like a child. When I became a man, I put childish ways behind me. Now we see but a poor reflection as in a mirror; then we shall see face to face. Now I know in part; then I shall know fully, even as I am fully known.

And now these three remain: **faith, hope and love**. But the greatest of these is **love**" *(1 Corinthians 13: 1-13)*

Chapter Thirty-One

Plan of Salvation

"Godly sorrow brings repentance that leads to salvation..."
(2 Corinthians 7: 10)
"For he says, "In the time of my favor I heard you,
and in the **day of salvation** I helped you. I tell you, now is
the time of God's favor, **now is the day of salvation**" (2
Corinthians 6:2)

You never have to grieve alone. "Believe in the Lord
Jesus, and you will be saved—you and your household"
(Acts 16:31) and there will always be someone who cares.

Prayer of Salvation

I believe that Jesus is the son of God, and that He died for
my sins. I'm sorry for my sins. Please forgive me. Come
into my heart and live in me. Save me, cleanse me, and
make me one of your own. In the name of Jesus, God's son,
I pray.

Sign name	Date of conversion

Just one drop of the blood Jesus spilled on the cross will wash away the pain, release all sin and guilt, and grant the ability to move ahead with joy and peace in your heart.

"...I will **forgive** their wickedness and will remember their sins no more" *(Hebrews 8:12)*

"Jesus said, "You have now seen him; in fact, he is the one speaking with you" *(John 9:37)*

Injustices and Forgiveness

"...forgive your brothers the sins and the wrongs they committed in treating you so badly..." *(Genesis 50:17)*

Looking back over a lifetime of injustices, heartache, disappointment, mistakes, regrets, and wrong decisions can make one re-think their objectives and goals. It's also important to take account of ourselves and purge our heart of any un-forgiveness, animosity, bitterness; even hatred toward others. Who can recognize our errors? Who can know our hidden thoughts?

"But blessed is the one who trusts in the Lord, whose confidence is in him. They will be like a tree planted by the water that sends out its roots by the stream. It does not fear when heat comes; its leaves are always green. It has no worries in a year of drought and never fails to bear fruit.

The heart is deceitful above all things and beyond cure. Who can understand it? I the Lord search the heart and examine the mind, to reward each person according to their conduct, according to what their deeds deserve" *(Jeremiah 17:7-10)*

But how do I overcome the injustices served me over a lifetime?

Forgiveness is the first step to re-thinking and re-designing our lives. Mercy for others is essential for healing and forgiveness. First we must forgive others for the wrongs done against us. Then we must forgive ourselves for harboring hatred and hostility towards them.

"...you ought to **forgive** and **comfort** him, so that he will not be overwhelmed by excessive **sorrow**"
(2 Corinthians 2:7)

"Bear with each other and **forgive** one another if any of you has a grievance against someone. **Forgive** as the Lord forgave you" *(Colossians 3:13)*

"Even if they sin against you seven times in a day and seven times come back to you saying 'I repent,' you must **forgive** them" *(Luke 17:4)*

"In him we have redemption through his blood, the forgiveness of sins, in accordance with the riches of God's grace" *(Ephesians 1:7)*

God's word will help us find healing and restoration, even in the most difficult of circumstances. Our prayer will then lead us on the path to forgiving others who've inflicted harsh wounds into our life.

"If we confess our sins, he is faithful and just and will **forgive** us our sins and purify us from all unrighteousness" *(1 John 1:9)*

Lastly, after we have forgiven others we must forgive ourselves. Only then will the weight of guilt melt into sheer freedom.

"So if the Son sets you free, you will be free indeed" *(John 8:36)*

And whatever effort it takes to achieve that freedom will have value beyond measure.

Chapter Thirty-Two

Fictional Narratives

Another way to grieve is by composing a narrative of relative significance. Then, after completion, your story may have a better ending than the one experienced following the loss of your loved one.

Writing fictional stories about similar circumstances was one way for me to alleviate many painful memories that followed the death of my son.

Often a story will simulate circumstances related to the deceased, or the desire for a different outcome. Unique expressions of sorrow may then offer an atypical spin concerning a different kind of sorrow. Either way, putting thoughts and feelings on paper can provide yet another facet of healing as you struggle to overcome personal grief and sorrow. A narrative can also be written as a way of addressing the issues of an empty or broken heart.

When life throws you a curve, it helps to journal those thoughts and feelings, therefore reducing the need to repress emotional distress. Disclosing the facts of your own grief with others may also help to lessen your own pain of sorrow.

Even if the story is fictional, it could aid in the healing process following the death of a loved one. But always remember, you're not alone. Others around the world are grieving with you.

✳✳✳

White Easter

"And we know that in all things God works for the good of those who love him, who have been called according to his purpose" *(Romans 8:28)*

The trim around the window framed feathery snowflakes as they cascaded gently to the ground from an overcast sky.

"Looks like we're having a white Easter this year," Deb said as she stood, hands on hips, and stared outside.

"Alright!" Austin said, then glanced at his mother before dashing to the window for a quick look outside. "Now we can hunt Easter eggs in the snow!"

"Not so fast," Jim said, then tousled his son's scruffy red hair head after joining him. "We have church this morning before Easter egg hunts."

"Oh yeah, I forgot," Austin said. Still staring outside, he scrunched his nose and scratched his head as snow continued to pile up around a thick rock wall just outside the window ledge.

Easter was early this year, coming in March instead of April as it had last year. Bright yellow daffodils in bloom next to the wall now cast wavy shadows on already fallen snow, and looked droopy and forlorn. But with the return of wintry weather, well Easter no longer looked, or felt, like a spring holiday. In fact, the outside air was so frigid, once the door was cracked open, chills would crawl up and down one's spine, and made them shiver.

***

Later that same day, as Austin sat on the sofa reading a comic book, the sound of a car door opening caught his attention. "Hey, Mom," he said. "Somebody's car just stopped outside." Then jumping from the sofa, he peered outside through the snow-streaked window. "Look. They're getting out and walking to the house."

A woman in her mid-thirty's holding the hand of a young girl began to slowly trudge up the snow-covered walkway; their shoes leaving a trail of shimmering footprints behind.

Austin turned and opened the door when the doorbell chimed. "Hello," he said, peering out.

"Hi. My name's Courtney, and this is my little girl Andrea. Our car just broke down and my cell phone died. Could I use your phone?"

"Mom," Austin said, his voice trailing. He then stepped aside, and Deb moved closer to the opened door.

Stepping closer, Courtney repeated her request; and immediately she and Andrea were invited inside the house.

"We've been traveling for two days on our way back to Florida, where we live." Courtney said, her voice meek and apologetic. "Andrea has leukemia. She had a doctor's appointment in Memphis at the cancer center for kids. But now my car's broken down and I don't have any money left to get it fixed. I don't know what I'm going to do."

Glancing up, Deb noted a look of despair on Courtney's face, and instantly realized the depth of the situation. "Don't worry about that right now," she said. "Take your jackets off, have some hot chocolate, and we'll figure out what to do."

"Why are you wearing that?" Austin asked, and pointed at a bright pink turban on Andrea's head.

"To hide my head," she said, looking down.

"She has leukemia," Courtney said again. "Her medication makes her hair fall out."

Meanwhile Jim had gone outside to have a look at the car. He then returned with his report.

"You have an oil leak for one thing," he said. "And, there seems to be a problem with the engine because it won't turn over. I'm no mechanic, but it's more than a dead battery. But the car garage is closed until Tuesday because of the holidays."

"Honey, can I talk to you for a minute?" Deb asked,

then pulled at Jim's arm, drawing him into the dining room.

"For some reason I feel like we should offer them a place to stay until Tuesday. Then she can get her car fixed. Maybe that's God speaking to me. What do you think?"

"Where would you put them?" Jim asked.

"The spare bedroom's always clean," Deb said.

"Is that what you really want to do?" Jim asked, his finger resting on his forehead.

"I feel like that's what God wants us to do," Deb said, then turned, and walked away.

In the living room Andrea was jumping up and down in excitement. "I've never seen snow before," she said.

"We've always been in Florida," Courtney said. "Memphis is as far as we've ever been from home. It's a long drive."

"Is the hospital helping Andrea?" Deb said, glancing down at the little girl.

"She's been sick for two years, since she turned three," Courtney said. "We don't know, but we're hoping."

"Can we go outside for a little while?" Andrea asked. "I want to touch the snow again."

"No, Andrea. It's too cold, and you've been sick." But when she noticed disappointment in her daughter's eyes, Courtney softened. "Well, maybe we will after all. Why not?"

Austin, Andrea, and Courtney then bundled up and went outside into a swirling mist of snowflakes.

"Let's build a snowman," Austin said, and grabbed a handful of snow. He then formed a ball from the white mixture, rolled it into a larger sphere, and placed it nearby to create the base of the snowman. Andrea, hands clasped in anticipation, stood by and giggled.

"This is better than hunting Easter eggs any old day," he said with a laugh.

"I know," she said, and then handed him another handful of the fluffy white stuff.

Later, and in record time, a gigantic snowman

emerged amid tons of churning white snowflakes. Still giggling, Andrea helped Austin dress their creation in an orange toboggan and green stripped scarf.

***

Early Tuesday morning, as the sun rose up over the horizon, a tow truck arrived—ready to drag Courtney's car to the service center for repairs. Later that same afternoon the car was returned in good running condition. Only minor repairs were needed after all.

The following morning as the travelers sat in their car ready for their return trip home, Courtney glanced through the car window one last time.

"I can't thank you enough for everything you've done for us," she said. "I couldn't have fixed my car, or anything else, without the help of this family. You were a God-send to us—a miracle."

"I'm just glad we could help," Deb said, and then gave her a quick hug through the window.

Courtney smiled, turned away, and quietly closed the window before turning the ignition key. Then slowly she backed down the slushy driveway.

"I hope we hear from you again." Deb said, her voice echoing back as they drove out of sight.

Five weeks later an envelope arrived in the mail. Then, as Deb ripped the seal, a clipped obituary page dropped to the ground. But when she saw the name 'Andrea' centered at the top of the page, she placed her hand on her heart and drew sharp breath

"Oh, no," she said. Then reaching down, she scooped up the page as tears formed, and dropped down on the clipping in her hand. The next instant a yellow sticky note, stuck to the top of the page, caught her attention. *Andrea's best day on earth was playing in the snow* was scribbled on it.

Again reaching up, she wiped more tears away. "You never know when you help someone what the outcome will be," she said out loud. "You just never know."

Brown Paper Bag
(A Mother's Day Story)

Robert wanted a son, but Rachael just wanted a child. She longed to be a mother, to feel the warmth of a child's embrace, and to know the love of a child no matter the cost.

Months later, after a long struggle with legal procedures, their application to adopt was approved; and they were ecstatic. Then, as a token of accomplishment, Rachael danced for joy and Robert snapped a picture to mark their achievement.

But with all the changes in their life, they were thankful Trevor's background of abuse and neglect hadn't made him timid or angry. Instead, his appreciation for positive attention kept him busy blowing kisses at Rachel with innocent abandonment. It was obvious he was grateful for a new start in his young life; and she was happy at last to be a mother.

Weeks later, following the adoption, they were ready to introduce their new son to his new grandparents. And Mother's Day seemed the perfect time for that introduction.

Sunday morning, after church was dismissed, they hurried to the car for a two hour drive. Rachael, voice resonating with joy, hummed the words of her favorite song as a brilliant sunshine scattered dazzling rays through a cloudless sky.

"Let's get some fresh mountain air," Robert said as he rolled his window down.

A wind-blown, wide-eyed Trevor then stared through the opening. "Are we there yet?" he asked.

"Not yet, but almost." Rachael said, brushing a few stray hairs from her face. "I know you're excited. I promise, it won't be long. Your new grandparents are probably as anxious as you are."

Later, as their van rolled into the driveway, Trevor bounced up and down in excitement. "Look, just look," he said, and pointed in the direction of his new grandma's flower garden. "Just look at all those flowers!"

Robert couldn't contain his laughter at Trevor's excitement as he helped him exit his car seat. Then turning, he smiled and waved at his in-laws as they walked toward them.

"Can I pick some? Please, please?" Trevor asked, looking straight at his new grandparents and holding both hands under his chin as if praying.

"No, I don't think so sweetie." Rachael said, and touched Trevor's arm in soft response. "These flowers are your grandma's prized flowers."

But the new grandma only smiled, and then gave Trevor a quick hug. "Today's a special day, and my new grandson can pick as many flowers as he wants," she said. Then looking directly at him, she pointed at the roses in her garden.

"But instead of picking handfuls of flowers, why don't you pick just one—a very special one for your new mommy for Mother's Day?" she asked.

Trevor again bounced up and down, and did an upside down flip while squealing in delight. Then pulling himself up, he turned and sprinted down a rock path that led to the colorful flower garden. But as he ran, he darted in and out of neatly staggered rows of red roses, yellow jonquils, and purple iris.

"Aren't you growing these flowers for a contest?" Rachael asked her mother.

"That doesn't matter," her mother said. "If it makes him happy, I don't care if he picks them all." Then stepping closer, she leaned over and whispered, "I'm glad you adopted him. He's such a delight to watch."

"It's okay for us to spoil him, isn't it?" The new grandpa asked, and then looked in the direction of his new grandson.

The next instant Trevor squealed loudly, and started running. "I got it," he said, panting. But, in his excitement, he tripped over a rock, and almost fell. "I got it," he said again, after regaining his balance. "I got the perfect flower for Mommy!"

Then ripping through the flower garden, and tripping over several jonquils and roses in his path, Trevor raced back to his new family. But held tightly in his grubby little hands was the largest sunflower in the garden—roots, dirt, and all.

"This is for you Mommy," he said, quite out of breath. "I got this one just for you." Still panting, he stopped dead in his tracks, right in front of his mother.

Rachael leaned forward, but gasped as Trevor, beaming with the pride of youth, thrust the enormous sunflower into her hands; dumping mud and crumbling clay onto her dress as the roots shed their residue.

"It's so big," she said, a little uncertain. But after holding the large plant in her hands, she realized how much Trevor must love her. And, with new understanding, she smiled and reached for him. Then drawing him close, and allowing her feelings to show, folded her arms around him in a bear hug.

"It's so beautiful," she whispered. "I love you so much." But as unexpected tears cascaded down her cheeks, she pressed Trevor even closer to her heart.

"Just look what God did," she said. "He made the perfect flower for you to give me on Mother's Day. But better yet, He made *you* just for me."

"I know," Trevor said, his grubby fingers stroking her arms. "I know."

Robert reached for his camera "We need a picture of this," he said, ready to snap another image for their photo album.

Rachael tried to smile through glistening tears as she held up a rather large sunflower with a now broken stem for the picture, her small protégé by her side.

***

Later that evening on the return trip home, Rachael turned and gazed at Robert as tears welled up in her eyes. "I'll never forget my first Mother's Day," she said. "It was just perfect."

"I totally agree," Robert said, then reached over to pat her on the knee. Still full of pride, he glanced around at Trevor, now asleep in his car seat.

"This *was* a perfect day," he said, "a picture perfect day."

***

Seventeen years later Rachael stood in silence as she examined the contents of a crisp paper bag the kind police officer handed her at the scene of a fatal car crash. There, on the bottom of the sack, lay a faded and somewhat weathered wallet.

With tender fingers she stroked the smooth texture of aged leather that had softened over time. Again lifting the shabby wallet to her face, she breathed in the faint aroma of her son as a wrinkled piece of paper slid silently to the ground.

Then bending over, she picked up a ragged picture of her beloved son as he handed her a rather large sunflower with a broken stem.

Chapter Thirty-Three

Mutual Understanding

November 1, 2009

J. Hannah: I've been thinking about you all week because I know it's now been five years since Dom went away. Today is not a celebration—nothing more to celebrate. It's a landmark, a milestone of sorrow.

I'll always feel your grief as you feel mine. We're bonded in a sisterhood of sadness because I know your pain, and grieve with you as you grieve with me.

Cathy: Thank you so much for your kind words. Whenever another mother talks to me who has lost a child, it's like they're inside my head. You know every emotion and how you go on in your life, but it is never the same. I can now see how people can die of a broken heart because the pain comes and goes and sometimes hits you at a time when you least expect. It just takes you down. Every once in a while the magnitude of Dom's loss hits me and it takes my breath away. I say to myself, "My God, he's real gone and I'll never see him in this life again." You can't wrap your head around it.

I sometimes wonder if other mothers, like you, don't really want to talk about it anymore, so I don't bring Dom up as much as I used to. His life is like a good movie that I have to keep replaying because there is no sequel; it's over. My daughter will say, "Remember when Dom did this or that," and that's how we keep him alive in our hearts. A couple of my friends had a mass said for Dom so we went to that which was nice and they also came. What I cannot believe is that my husband's sisters did not call, e-mail, or anything to say they were thinking of him! I know he was hurt as he mentioned it to me. I was aware of it, but didn't want to bring it up. Sometimes family is the most disappointing of all.

Thanks for being there for me. I appreciate it more than you know. It's amazing how people like us just happened to come in contact with because of our shared sadness, are the kindest of all. I always say I belong to a sad club and I don't want any more members.

May 19, 2010

Cathy: Isn't it amazing how the time goes by when you're a parent? One minute they are starting kindergarten and the next thing you know they want the keys to the car. Sometimes I wish I could live my life in reverse. I'm still appreciative of things in life, but it just never gets back to where it should be when you lose a child. There's always this hole you're trying to fill. Sometimes when we go out to eat it hits me that we are sitting there, three instead of four.

I imagine what it would feel like to have Dom walk through the door and sit with us again. I see Dom's sister, cousins, and friends going on with their lives and it can't help but sting a little. It will hit me at the oddest times and I find myself crying. The other day I was in the shower and broke down for no reason at all. Losing a child is a wound that never quite heals.

J. Hannah: You said it all. The other day when I got home I noticed a young man walking in the distance. He was the same stature as Matthew, looked like him, and was dressed in a similar way. And, he was wearing a baseball cap. Matt always wore one. My heart missed a beat. Then that awful feeling hit me in the gut and made me sick. To make matters worse, I was listening to that song by Michael

Buble called *Home.* I cried my eyes out. Have you heard that song?

Cathy: Oh, J. Hannah ...that song by Michael Buble always makes me think of Dom and it rips me apart!! It's a beautiful song, but sometimes when it comes on the radio, I have to change the channel because I can't handle it. It always makes me think, maybe Dom is looking down on us and wishing he could be here for all the changes that have happened; but, then according to what I've read, they are at perfect peace.

I sure wouldn't want him to be looking back and feeling sad. I do wonder though if he misses us at times like we miss him. I wonder, with no time or space, what do you do? Where do you go? What is this after life? I can't imagine not having an earthly body to contend with. So many crazy questions go through your head when you lose someone. All we can do is speculate as to what it's like.

It's always good to be able to talk to you like this. It gives me some peace because I know you understand.

Chapter Thirty-Four

Moving Forward

At some point following the death of a loved one the harshness of sorrow will soften, but it may take months, even years before that happens. In the meantime it's best to allow the amount of time needed to process the details of your loss. Although the course may be difficult to maneuver, peace and happiness will again come. Sorrow and pain are but for a season as God desires each of us to live our lives to the fullest.

"Weeping may endure for a night but joy comes in the morning" *(Psalms 30:5)*

Without a doubt, trials and death are part of the sequence. Still, losing a loved one will be difficult to accept, if not impossible, for a time. Many have said they will carry their sorrow to the grave.

It's expected that a parent will pass when they are old. It's also understandable that a spouse will one day die. But it's not reasonable for a parent to outlive a child.

Having to accept the death of someone you hold dear will eventually happen. But when that moment comes, allow God to be your traveling companion. With His help and the help of others, the hurdle of grief is survivable with grace and peace in your heart.

"My **comfort** in my suffering is this: Your promise preserves my life" *(Psalms 119:50)*

Conclusion

End of the Road

"Come to me, all you who are weary and burdened, and I will give you rest. Take my yoke upon you and learn from me, for I am gentle and humble in heart, and you will find rest for your souls" *(Matthew 11:28, 29)*

Many times I needed restoration from despair, anger, and all my hurts. But, I wasn't receptive. The hurt was just too deep. After all, I was the one who was in control. I could handle it. Those offenses were part of who I was.

Medicine hadn't worked. Well, it did help for the short haul. But long term it was just another crutch—an addiction without a cure.

I was tired. I was weary. And, my strength was almost gone. My will to live was dying too. That never-ending road ahead was full of curves and potholes. I was just too worn out for the journey.

What could I do now? I was at the end of the road, ready to jump off a bridge and end it all; to be done with my life. What was left for me? I was out of options. Stuck in a rut, weathered and exhausted, I struggled with my decision.

Then, as a last resort, I picked up the Bible, and opened it. And immediately verses of restoration and words of hope leaped off the page and into my spirit.

"Come to me, all you who are weary and burdened, and I will give you rest" *(Matthew 11:28)*

But exactly what did that mean? Reading further I found the answer.

Give the depression, the sorrow, and the heartache to God. Release the pain, the hurt, and the anger. Let go of all bitterness and allow the burden of grief to rest on the shoulders of the One who's big enough to carry it.

"You will not have to fight this battle. Do not be afraid; do not be discouraged. For the battle is not yours, but God's..." *(2 Chronicles 20: 17, 15)*

Set it free, give it to God; and let it go.

And, I did.

"He who dwells in the shelter of the Most High will rest in the shadow of the Almighty" *(Psalms 91:1)*

"'May God give you of heaven's dew and of earth's richness" (Genesis 27:28)

Credits

Grieving God's Way by Margaret Brownley
He Held My Hand by Deborah Morocco Mason
Mourning and Melancholia (1917), Sigmund Freud
After a Child Dies by Harold K. Bush, Jr.
All scripture in Death Came Quickly was taken from the New International Version of the Bible unless otherwise indicated.
www.jhannahlloyd.com

Abbreviations

A.S. Asperger Syndrome

Bibliography

Mourning and Melancholia (1917) Sigmund Freud Freud, Sigmund. (1916-1917g [1915]) "Trauer und Melancholie," *Intern. Zschr. ärztl. Psychoanal 4*, p. 277-287; *G.W.*, 10, 428-448; Mourning and melancholia. *SE*, 14: 243-258.

Grieving God's Way ©.Copyright 2004 Margaret Brownley

Zondervan Bible New International Version Copyright 1973, 1978, 1984 by International Bible Society® The Zondervan Corporation Grand Rapids, MI 49530 U.S.A.

New International Version, ©2011 (NIV) Copyright © 1973, 1978, 1984, 2011 by *Biblica*

It is well with my soul *Words:* Horatio G. Spafford, 1873. *Music:* VILLE DU HAVRE, Philip P. Bliss, in *Gospel Hymns No. 2*, by P. P. Bliss & Ira D. Sankey (New York: Biglow & Main, 1876), number 76 (*note:* published in a combined volume with the 1875 *Gospel Hymns and Sacred Songs*) (MIDI, NWC, PDF). Ironically, Bliss himself died in a train wreck shortly after writing this music.

Dictionary.com, LLC. Copyright © 2011
www.dictionary.com
Scarlett O'Hara, a character from Margaret Mitchell's 1936
novel Gone with the Wind

Grief Resources

http://www.griefshare.org/
http://grief.net/
http://www.missionsinternational.org/store.htm

Resources

Andrew Wommack, www.awmi.net

Ann Tatlock – www.anntatlock.com

Billy Graham's *The Cove* – (800) 950-2092 or visit
www.thecove.org. Billy Graham Training Center

Cheryl Salem, www.salemfamilyministries.org

Deborah Morocco Mason – Book, He Held my Hand
http://www.missionsinternational.org/store.htm

Del Way, http:www.delway.org

Grief Share, www.griefshare.org – help in finding a
location in your area that offers help for grief recovery

Vonda Skelton – Author of *Seeing through the Lies:
Unmasking the Myths Women Believe* and *The Bitsy
Burroughs Mysteries* - www.VondaSkelton.com
www.vondaskelton.com Speaker

Yvonne Lehman, Founder of Lifeway Blue Ridge
Mountains Christian Writer's Conference, Ridgecrest,
North Carolina; director of Blue Ridge "Summer" and

"Autumn" novel retreats and author of 50 novels. www.yvonnelehman.com

Contributors

Ann Tatlock - Novelist and Author of the award winning Christy award, *All the Way Home.* www.anntatlock.com

Belle Woods – www.bellwoods.blogspot.com

Austin Allen

Carolyn Knefely - Speaker, etiquette specialist and career coach, people polisher and co-director of Christian Communicators www.teacupliving.blogspot.com

Cathy Pendola

Lori Marett - Co-founder Gideon Film Festival www.gideonfilmfestival.com

Cindy Sproles - Christian Devotions Ministries - P.O. Box 6494 - Kingsport, TN 37663, christiandevotions.us, www.iBegat.com, DevoKids.com, www.DevoFest.com, devocionescristiano.com blogtalkradio.com/Christian-Devotions

Endorsements

"Life as it had been would never be the same again." Those pain-filled words come from J. Hannah Lloyd's heart in her book *Death Came Quickly*. She knows from experience that we each have times in our lives when we grieve over one or many losses. She knows first-hand that grieving is necessary and a process. Can we reach the other side of grief to a brighter day? Can we let go? Blame God? Or trust Him? Can we reach out to others who are grieving?

Her book has the answer to those and many questions, and incorporates her own message of hope for hurting hearts.

—YVONNE LEHMAN
Author "summer" and "autumn" novel retreats   and author of 50 novels. Her latest release is *Aloha Brides*, a collection of historical novels set in Hawaii.

J. Hannah Lloyd is a shining example of one who is able to comfort just as she herself has been comforted (2 Corinthians 1:4). I know, because I've seen it not only in her written words, but in her life. She exudes a solid faith and an unyielding peace that comes only from journeying to the deepest places of grief and finding God there. Now, through her writing, her poetry, and her insights, she walks beside you on your own journey through grief, encouraging and supporting you every step of the way.

—ANN TATLOCK
Award-winning novelist

Some people go places others only dream of going. But others have to go *through* places that, for most, are simply 'nightmares'. J. Hannah Lloyd speaks of traveling through such a place; and yet finds help and healing in the darkest of valleys as she walks with the Good Shepherd. In *Death Came Quickly* she shares her source of strength with hurting souls; not simply from head knowledge but from a heart that has lived it.

—JERRY D. MADDEN,
Sr. Pastor – Praise Cathedral
Greer, SC

Acknowledgments

A special thanks to:

Ann Tatlock, a personal friend, for guiding me into the world of professional writing. She is a personal friend and one of my first mentors. Our friendship began when my friend Bonnie introduced us at a Women's Bible Study at Billy Graham's *The Cove* located in Asheville, North Carolina. Because of this introduction Ann invited me to the Blue Ridge Mountain's Christian Writer's Conference in Ridgecrest, North Carolina. This conference and several more, coupled with Ann's confidence in my work, gave me the assurance I needed to pursue the writing of this book on grief. Our friendship is ongoing and a testimony to how God works out the details of our lives through others.

Bonnie Lowdermilk, now deceased, was my best friend from childhood until her death in 2007. Her encouragement helped push me into a writing career when she introduced me to Ann Tatlock.

Austin Allen, my middle child and oldest son, for his willingness to write about his feelings of remorse following the death of his sibling, and for his assistance in helping me recall childhood antics of his brother Matthew. Several memories inspired personal stories that are scattered throughout the pages of *Death Came Quickly*.

Carolyn K. Knefely for her friendship and willingness to write her story in *Death Came Quickly* about the infant daughter she lost years ago. Her narrative offers hope and healing to others who've lost a baby in death.

Alison McCall, a personal friend who shared her story with me following the loss of both her youngest son, and her husband. Her strength is amazing, as she continues her journey into healing.

Cathy Pendola, for her willingness to write her story that details the tragic loss her son Dominic. We met online through a mutual friend of a friend shortly after the death of her son. Matt had been dead about three months when we began our E-mail communication. Our online friendship has continued for over seven years. Together we worked through much of the grieving process. She remains a solid rock for me. Her stories are dynamic and heartfelt.

Cindy Sproles, a personal friend who continues to inspire many by providing daily devotionals on www.ChristianDevotions.us; a website she created for the Internet. Cindy's devotional *Bring Them Home* is included in *Death Came Quickly*, and has great meaning in an essential chapter.

My husband of over twenty-four years, step-father of my children, and great supporter of my writing craft. His love, sensitivity, and assistance provided ongoing support for the writing of this book.

Lori Marett, who took the time to edit my manuscript, suggest placement of chapters, and offer ideas to further develop the content of *Death Came Quickly*. Her contributed stories provide valid points and profound insight. Her belief that I could accomplish this work was one of the catalysts that spurred me forward. Lori is a personal friend and expert editor.

Belle Woods, a personal friend and devoted Christian. Her willingness to write about the death of her husband provides significant insight in *Death Came Quickly*. Her devotion to the memory of her husband will relate to others who've also lost a spouse through death.

Yvonne Lehman, a personal friend, and one of my first mentors who drew me into a fold of writers through her support group. She critiqued many of my stories while encouraging me to be published. Her friendship and support will always be appreciated.

J. Hannah Lloyd

About the Author

J. Hannah Lloyd is an author, poet, and free-lance writer who currently lives in South Carolina with her husband and two demanding felines.

In 2007 she was presented two awards for her work at the Blue Ridge Mountain Christian Writer's Conference in Ridgecrest, North Carolina. As a poet and writer, her articles, stories, and poetry have been published in adult and children's Christian literature as well as online.

Other works have been published in Slate & Style, Shemom, Harold and Banner Press in Primary Pal: Pacific Press Publishing Association in Our Little Friend, MS Focus and MS Connection Magazines, Who's DANN?—a monthly magazine, Gospel Publishing House in LIVE; a weekly journal; the Pentecostal Evangel—an Assemblies of God publication, Heartland Boating, Critter Magazine, Wilderness Grace—a newsletter, and the Upper Room magazine.

Visit her online at www.jhannahlloyd.com and www.survivordynamics.wordpress.com

Other books by the Author

Tied to Terror-Secrets of a Battered Wife
Escape from Abuse Survival Guide
Dead Man's Curve-The Crossing

Proof

Made in the USA
Charleston, SC
12 August 2014